ACPL ITEM
DISCARDED

336
Soli
SOVEREIGN RESCHEDULING

S0-BWX-537

3 1833 01904 9110

336.3435 So4s
SOLBERG, RONALD L., 1953-
SOVEREIGN RESCHEDULING

ALLEN COUNTY PUBLIC LIBRARY

FORT WAYNE, INDIANA 46802

You may return this book to any agency, branch,
or bookmobile of the Allen County Public Library.

Sovereign Rescheduling
Risk and
Portfolio Management

Sovereign Rescheduling

**Risk and
Portfolio Management**

RONALD L. SOLBERG

London
UNWIN HYMAN
Boston   Sydney   Wellington

© International Economic Consultants, 1988
This book is copyright under the Berne Convention.
No reproduction without permission. All rights reserved.

Published by the Academic Division of
Unwin Hyman Ltd
15/17 Broadwick Street, London W1V 1FP

Allen & Unwin Inc.,
8 Winchester Place, Winchester, Mass. 01890, USA

Allen & Unwin (Australia) Ltd,
8 Napier Street, North Sydney, NSW 2060, Australia

Allen & Unwin (New Zealand) Ltd
in association with the Port Nicholson Press Ltd
60 Cambridge Terrace, Wellington, New Zealand

First published in 1988

Allen County Public Library
Ft. Wayne, Indiana

British Library Cataloguing in Publication Data

Solberg, Ronald L.
    Sovereign rescheduling: risk and portfolio management.
1. Debts, External   2. Debts, Public
3. Risk
I. Title
336.3'6   HJ8015
ISBN 0–04–332122–4

Library of Congress Cataloging-in-Publication Data

Solberg, Ronald L., 1953–
    Sovereign rescheduling: risk and portfolio management/Ronald L.
Solberg.
"Extension of . . . PhD dissertation written at the University of
California, Berkeley, from 1981 to 1984"—Acknowledgements.
Bibliography: p.
Includes index.
ISBN 0–04–332 122–4 (alk. paper)
1. Loans, Foreign.   2. Debt relief.   3. Country risk.   4. Portfolio
management.   5. Intermediation (Finance)   I. Title
HB3891.5.S65 1988
336.3'435—dc19

Typeset in 10 on 11 point Times by Phoenix Photosetting, Chatham
and printed in Great Britain by Billing and Son Ltd, London
and Worcester

Contents

List of Tables

List of Figures

This book is dedicated to my parents,
Carl and Gladys

Acknowledgements

This book is an extension of my PhD. dissertation written at the University of California, Berkeley, from 1981 to 1984; thus it is appropriate that I extend my thanks and gratitude to those on my dissertation committee who intellectually and morally supported my research. The immediate committee consisted of John M. Letiche, Laura D'Andrea Tyson, both of the Economics Department, and Robert Price of the Political Science Department. I would also like to thank Gregory Grossman and Henry Brady for offering valuable advice and support during this period. Funding for the dissertation research was generously provided by the Institute of International Studies and the Department of Economics, University of California at Berkeley.

As the final form of this book has taken shape, I have continued to receive stimulating input from my colleagues and friends in the financial and academic communities. Brian Newton of BARRA generously contributed his expert assistance, helping to update the data base and rerun much of the regression work during the rewriting of the manuscript. In addition, I wish to make particular mention of Lee Ohanian, Charles Semones and Jeff Shaw both of Security Pacific National Bank; Tom Hedden of the University of California at Berkeley; David Beers of Salomon Brothers; Don Winkler of the University of Southern California and the World Bank; Jim Devine of Loyola Marymount University and Prem Thapa of Integrated Development Systems, Nepal. At the same time, regular contact and stimulating discussions with my graduate students at the University of Southern California, many of whom come from the developing world, have served as a continual reminder of the pressing needs and concerns of their countries.

Last but not least, I wish to thank my wife, Anna, for her logistical support and patience during my extended preoccupation with this manuscript.

The opinions expressed in this book are solely those of the author and do not represent the views of either the Security Pacific National Bank or the University of Southern California. Naturally, responsibility for errors of omission or commission remain those of the author alone.

Preface

The purpose of this book is to obtain a clearer understanding of why the international financial intermediation process broke down after 1982, how this knowledge can be used to build a more efficient predictor of sovereign debt rescheduling probabilities, and finally to explain how this model can be used to minimize risk. Its applications include the objective allocation of new international loans, the minimization of non-systematic, that is, country-specific, risk within a creditor's portfolio, pricing new international sovereign loans and determining the value of impaired sovereign loans in the secondary market. Wider application of these principles will help to deepen the secondary market for developing country debt, facilitating debt-for-debt and debt-for-equity swaps and identifying arbitrage opportunities. By spreading the current risks amongst a wider array of creditors, this financial deepening should help to improve the stability of the international financial markets.

The integrated approach found in this book is in large measure a reflection of my own personal history. The ideas expressed here germinated during the halcyon lending days of the late 1970s when, after graduate studies at the University of California, Berkeley, I accepted a position in the City of London. As the Country Risk Analyst, covering Western and Eastern Europe and the Middle East for an American bank, I was in regular contact with both the policy-makers in those regions and with key managers in the institutions providing them with funds. It was this opportunity to observe and contribute to the process by which financial capital flowed from the developed to the developing countries that prompted my return to my *alma mater* with the intention of testing the theoretical framework presented here.

While I was engrossed with my research, the debt crisis continued to intensify. My manuscript complete, I devoted myself to analysing Pacific Basin economies for another major bank, as the creditworthiness of an increasing number of once 'financially sound' debtors was being called into question. The world financial community with the assistance of key multilateral agencies, subsequently found a *modus operandi* which enabled them to postpone, and perhaps avoid, widespread defaults, that is, legal repudiation, by developing countries. As a result of this disruption, both public and private institutions had, however, come under much greater scrutiny and this has continued to place further pressure on the level of their assistance. Given these developments, I was reluctant to publish any econometric results without extending my data base to incorporate this latest phase in the recycling saga. Accordingly, the model presented in this book has been re-estimated, and found to hold true, for an expanded time period covering sixty-seven debtor countries from 1971 to 1984.

Part I reviews the developments within the global economy which set the stage for the dramatic increase in cross-border liabilities of the developing world during the 1970s. The financial intermediation process as it developed in the 1970s, its subsequent dislocation in the 1980s, and the attendant risks are outlined here.

Part II views international financial intermediation from the perspective of the lender. Contemporary credit-scoring models of sovereign debt rescheduling risk are reviewed and the difficulties of developing and testing such models are discussed.

Based on the postulated behaviour of a sovereign debtor, a new credit-scoring model is constructed in Part III and shown to be a useful debt early warning system to assess prospective sovereign creditworthiness. Developed from a Lancaster-type utility framework, this logit model incorporates liquidity, adjustment and solvency criteria as explanatory variables. The model explains why the illiquid and perhaps insolvent debtor, facing increasingly limited policy options and a rising relative cost of sustained borrowing versus debt service payment arrears, saw rescheduling as a rational choice.

The results show that the global risk of rescheduling almost doubled between the early 1970s and the early 1980s. The external pressures were felt most keenly by those countries which exhibited poor asset-liability management and an inadequate stabilization programmes in response to a myriad of external shocks. In particular, insufficient adjustment of the real exchange rate to these shocks was a common attribute. Solvency and credit cost factors also came into play for those debtors that ignored or incorrectly applied prudent principles of development planning and investment allocation in using borrowed funds. The importance of prior rescheduling performance as a predictive variable implies that credit supply constraints were also an important determinant of rescheduling behaviour.

The belated preoccupation of many developing countries with immediate needs of foreign exchange liquidity impaired their ability to ease the very medium and long-term constraints to growth which had made them so vulnerable to disturbances in the world economy.

As expected, the results confirm that the low income countries initially ran the highest risks of rescheduling. Towards the end of the sample period, however, the high income developing countries and the net-oil exporters found their range of available policy options similarly reduced in the face of new external shocks, thus significantly heightening their rescheduling probabilities.

Chapter 7 shows how the results of the credit-scoring model can be used effectively by any international creditor institution to reduce the overall risk of its portfolio by actively managing country credit limits. Given the projected country-specific rescheduling probabilities, the model also can be used to price new or impaired international financial assets. At the same time, the model serves as a useful tool for developing countries in determining the optimal amount of foreign capital needed to balance sustained development goals with ensured continual access to external credit markets.

During the first quarter of 1987, the debt crisis was heightened with the announcement that Brazil, the largest developing country debtor, would suspend interest payments on debt owed to foreign commercial banks. When a portion of these responded by cutting short-term credit lines, Brazil reacted quickly by freezing additional trade credits and interbank deposits.

Although the Brazilian actions may be indicative of a key juncture in the ongoing evolution of the debt crisis, this or any escalation of financial brinksmanship benefits no member of the international financial community; it simply threatens stability. The lasting solution requires the stabilization and reduction of the real debt burden through increased international trade and economic growth. This necessitates renewal of a positive net financial transfer to developing countries and a more diverse group of international creditors lending at more predictable rates. This book, by offering an efficient predictor of sovereign debt rescheduling probability and presenting its various applications to reducing the spreading risks in the international capital markets, is intended to make a modest contribution toward solving the current impasse in international financial intermediation.

Mar Vista, Los Angeles   *Ronald L. Solberg*
March, 1987

The Rise and Fall of International Lending:

An Overview of the Global Debt Crisis, 1973 to the Present

1.
Increasing Risks in the Global Recycling Process, 1973–1981

1.1 Introduction

The positive contribution of foreign savings (or external capital inflow) to the process of economic development and growth had been an accepted tenet of academicians, policy-makers, and businessmen for much of the 1950s, 1960s and 1970s. It was thought that efficient use of foreign (fiduciary, fixed, or human) capital could accelerate the domestic investment programme, transfer advanced technology, improve production, distribution, and organizational methods and increase access to international markets.

During the 1950s and 1960s the amount of external borrowing by developing countries was primarily an endogenous policy decision based on the borrower's savings and investment behaviour. Much of the research on economic development and the allocation of international aid flows during the post-war era has been underpinned by these assumptions.[1]

During the 1970s, however, factors other than the pace and composition of economic growth must be identified as determining the rapid growth of international debt. The pricing clout of the Organization of Petroleum Exporting Countries (OPEC) cartel, stagflation in the major industrial countries and the rise of trade protectionism all resulted in large exogenous increases in the demand for external credit by developing country borrowers. In addition, key supply-side trends, such as the abandonment of the Bretton Woods agreement on fixed exchange rates and the growth of the international capital markets, have produced asymmetries in international trade and investment flows. All these factors created large and persistent current account imbalances and adjustment difficulties for developing countries during the 1970s. Such changes in the international economic environment increased the exogeneity or the externally-induced component of foreign capital requirements for developing countries. This accelerated the growth of debt and contributed to the rapidly changing character of international financial intermediation since 1973. These changes, together with the inadequate policy response of the debtor countries themselves, at a time when the commercial banks were becoming increasingly reluctant to continue lending to developing countries on a large scale, dramatically increased the incidence of debt rescheduling cases during the 1980s.

The scope and magnitude of the recent debt problem has made many developing country policy-makers and academic economists increasingly sceptical of the role which foreign capital can play in the development process. This attitude is reinforced by the relative paucity of voluntary international lending by the private financial institutions and the inadequate amounts of new money currently being supplied by the multilateral and bilateral lending agencies.

1.2   The Origins of International Lending to Developing Countries

The OPEC oil price increases of 1973–74 and industrial country stagflation were fundamental determinants of the dramatic rise in developing country external debt since 1973. Additionally, the rise of new trade protectionism, and the collapse of the Bretton Woods system resulted in the absence of an effective global adjustment mechanism which accentuated the necessity for cross-border capital flows. The massive financial intermediation underpinning this rapid growth was made possible by key supply side factors. Of greatest importance were the growth and integration of the international capital markets and the increased supply of international liquidity. Thus, the origins of the rapid growth of international lending to the developing countries during the 1970s must be traced to events which began in the 1960s or earlier.

The Rise of Global Capital Markets

In the period of the cold war during the early 1950s, the Eurodollar market was formed when Eastern European banks deposited US dollars in Western European banks, attempting to avoid having their assets frozen by the US government. This offshore dollar market remained small, however, until the major European currencies became convertible in 1957 and the European Economic Community (EEC) was formed in 1958. Increased trade and financial flows, both within the EEC and between the EEC and the United States, in turn, increased the transactions-demand and asset-demand for the US dollar. While growing rapidly, the Eurodollar market remained small with gross liabilities valued at US $20 billion at year-end 1964 (Morgan Guaranty Trust Company, 1976). During the next decade, the market's growth was sustained primarily by the imposition of US capital controls between 1963 and 1968, and by large US external borrowing in 1969.[2] These events in the 1950s and 1960s resulted in demand-led growth for a dollar-based financial market outside the United States. In the 1970s, the growth of the Eurodollar market was driven by supply-side factors.[3]

The magnitude of OPEC's export revenue in 1974 was more than could be absorbed in current purchases of imported goods and services by the oil-exporting countries. Thus it was the disposition of the OPEC surplus in the form of financial deposits which fuelled the growth of the Euromarkets after 1973. According to the International Monetary Fund (IMF 1983b), OPEC deposited US $111 billion in the Eurocurrency market during the years 1974–1982, representing 26.3 per cent of their cumulative surplus. By 1982, gross liabilities in the Eurocurrency market were estimated at US $2.0 trillion, with net liabilities valued at approximately US $900 billion. At that time over 70 per cent of this amount was denominated in US dollars.

The size and efficiency of the Eurocurrency market facilitated the huge financial intermediation effort which was required by the large payments imbalances between deficit and surplus countries after the first oil-price shock. It is unlikely that the bilateral and multilateral financial institutions alone would have been able to recycle the volume of funds which the world payments system required in the 1970s. If global financial intermediation had been inadequate it is likely the 1974–75 OECD recession would have been deeper and prolonged.

The magnitude of the recycling effort was enormous. While OPEC's direct loans and grants to the non-oil developing countries represented only 7.4 per cent of the oil exporters' combined current account surplus in 1974, the non-oil developing countries' current account deficit represented 56.9 per cent of the OPEC surplus. Thus, an equivalent of 49.5 per cent of OPEC's surplus had to be recycled to the non-oil developing countries alone. In the highly competitive Eurocurrency market, the absence of regulation may have contributed to an erosion of prudent lending standards.[4]

In 1974, immediately after the first oil price shock, even the OECD countries ran a current account deficit of US $26.0 billion (OECD, 1983a). During the years 1975–1978 the industrial countries were able to adjust resources so as to regain a current account surplus. Eastern Europe and the non-oil developing countries, however, continued to run large, even growing current account deficits. Without an adequate global adjustment mechanism after the collapse in 1971 of the Bretton Woods agreement, huge payments imbalances persisted, requiring ongoing developing country debt accumulation.

Collapse of the Bretton Woods System of Fixed Exchange Rates
The end of the US dollar's official link to gold and the advent of managed floating exchange rates in 1971 tended to exert deflationary pressures on the global economic environment. By increasing the uncertainty over future exchange-rate values this, in turn, contributed to a deceleration in the growth of world trade. Having averaged an annual compound rate of 8.5 per cent during the years 1963–1972, the real growth of world trade fell to only 4.0 per cent per annum from 1973 to 1982 (IMF, 1983b).

The absence of an explicit adjustment mechanism meant that disequilibria in the balance of payments were more exaggerated and persistent. The annual average deficit in the balance of trade for the industrialized countries and the non-oil developing countries during 1963–1972 was US $6.3 billion and US $11.6 billion, respectively. These average annual imbalances rose to US $58.2 billion and US $56.2 billion, respectively, in the period from 1973–1982 (IMF, 1982b and 1985c).

Hallwood and Sinclair (1981) have argued that the new regime of managed floating exchange rates after 1971 meant that countries could no longer 'run their economies with a high pressure of demand'. The United States and the United Kingdom had to be more cautious about running their economies at full capacity. If they financed their current account deficits by exporting their reserve currencies, currency depreciation could result.

Thus after 1971, other industrial countries could pursue a slower growth path resulting in current account surpluses and an appreciating currency. Such a slow growth strategy would avoid importing the inflationary pressures from the reserve currency countries. Notably, the anti-inflationary policies of West Germany and Japan led to large current account surpluses, appreciating currencies, and rapidly rising international reserves. Thus, flexible exchange rates reduced the inherent tendency of industrialized countries toward full employment demand management policies which had existed under the Bretton Woods System.

The sum of the value of the current account for all surplus countries, plus the sum of the value of the current account for all the deficit countries, should equal zero, ignoring such technical factors as the annual monetization of gold, differences in accounting practices and smuggling. This variant of Say's law highlights the policy interdependence of global trade adjustment. Given this global interdependence of trade adjustment policies and the tendency of certain strong economies to run persistently large current account surpluses after the collapse of the Bretton Woods agreement, it became more difficult for the non-oil developing countries to implement a successful stabilization programme to lower their trade deficits. This required the developing countries to resort to external debt accumulation rather than trade adjustment as the primary policy response to the OPEC supply shock.

The OPEC Cartel and Industrial Country Stagflation
Besides the immediate effect of redistributing world income, the OPEC price increases also resulted in slower growth of world output and trade, necessitating greater reliance on debt accumulation as a developing country policy response. Park (1976) has argued that the oil price shock raised the global saving rate by increasing the income of countries with a relatively lower marginal propensity to consume. Thus, the slower growth of global aggregate demand would introduce a deflationary bias for the growth of output, employment and world trade.

The macroeconomic performance of the industrial countries after the oil price shock of 1973/74 has been well below their performance of the prior two decades. Stagflation, characterized by slower growth of output and stubbornly high inflation coupled with rising levels of unemployment, has been a persistent problem for the OECD countries since the early 1970s. During the years 1960–1973, the growth of gross domestic product (GDP) in the OECD countries averaged an annual rate of 4.9 per cent. Inflation, as measured by the consumer price index, increased an average of 3.9 per cent per annum (OECD, 1983a). Between 1973–1979 by comparison, the growth of GDP decelerated to an average 2.7 per cent per annum, while the rate of consumer price inflation increased to an annual average of 10.0 per cent (OECD, 1983a). After having averaged 3.2 per cent during 1960–1973, the average unemployment rate in the Organization for Economic Cooperation and Development (OECD) countries jumped to 5.5 per cent during 1974–1981 (OECD, 1983a).

The increase in the price of oil (for example, Saudi Arabian Ras Tanura from US $1.90 per barrel in 1972 to US $32.50 per barrel in 1981) certainly contributed to the decline in OECD performance (IMF, 1985c). The policy response of most OECD countries was to implement deflationary economic policies to control inflation and reduce the current account deficit. The increased uncertainty surrounding investment opportunities, owing to higher production costs (oil price and the wage-price spiral) and weakening markets, tended to lower aggregate demand even more. The higher oil price level also made a portion of the existing energy intensive capital stock obsolete. Hence, the oil price shock not only caused an immediate reduction in, and slower growth of, aggregate demand but also narrowed the base of productive capital. As a result, there were some dramatic changes on the supply side and structural unemployment increased.

In summary, the primary impact of the oil price shock was to increase the flow of real and financial resources among countries, requiring an unprecedented degree of global financial intermediation. The secondary impact of OPEC pricing policy exacerbated OECD stagflation. The inability of policy-makers in the developed countries to aggressively pursue positive adjustment policies, in turn, worsened the trade and adjustment prospects for the developing countries.

Positive Adjustment Policies and the New Trade Protectionism

The stagflation and rising unemployment levels in OECD countries during the 1970s diminished their capacity to shed declining industries. The international comparative advantage of the textiles, footwear, shipbuilding, coal and steel industries in the developed countries shifted to lower-cost economies. Socioeconomic rigidities diminished the willingness of the developed countries to pursue structural change or positive adjustment policies (OECD, 1983b). The growing proportion of public enterprise or government subsidies in total output, changes in the factor markets, the large fixed costs of investment and political alliances between the declining industries and strong labour unions all impeded the dismantling of high-cost industries and slowed the move into new technologies.

These rigidities led to the rise of the new trade protectionism. Non-tariff barriers significantly hindered the ability of the developing countries, particularly the newly industrializing countries (NICs), to penetrate the developed markets.[5] The rising trade barriers in the OECD countries further diminished the trade adjustment capability of the developing countries, increasing their reliance on external debt accumulation and lowering their creditworthiness.

According to the 'product cycle' theory of international trade (Vernon, 1966), changes over time in the cost structure or input requirements of a product will shift the comparative advantage of production from higher cost to lower cost countries. The location of production, by seeking the most cost-efficient operating environment, will gravitate toward lower-income labour-surplus countries. This process allows the labour surplus developing countries to inherit important lines of production which, in a free trading environment, will hasten their economic growth and development. The counterpart of the 'product cycle' for the developed countries is that government policies encourage structural change. Positive adjustment policies would entail the dismantling of declining industries where unskilled-labour-intensive techniques are being used in a high-cost country. Government-funded employment reorientation, including job training, tax incentives for research and development and new technology-intensive investment would encourage a more rapid shift toward higher value-added production.

In an ideal world, the smooth cross-border diffusion of production processes would facilitate faster growth of world output. Not only would foreign investment and world trade increase as the comparative advantage shifted across countries, but, by ensuring that all countries had the opportunity to move into higher value-added production, incomes would rise and GNP growth accelerate in both developed and developing countries alike.

1.3 International Capital Flows and Non-Oil Developing Country Debt

After 1973, the demand and supply side factors outlined in Section 1.2 hindered the non-oil developing countries in their attempts to narrow their external resource gap. Table 1.1 shows that the current account deficit for this group increased more than threefold in 1974 and remained on a rising trend through 1981. While accumulation of foreign exchange reserves, capital flight and the extension of export credits also contributed to this resource gap, the growing current account deficit was the largest component, ranging from 57 per cent to 92 per cent of gross borrowing requirements during this period.[6]

The Acceleration of External Debt Growth
Although non-debt-creating flows such as foreign direct investment, official transfers (that is, foreign aid) and allocations of Special Drawing Rights increased from 1973 to 1981, their rate of growth did not keep pace with overall borrowing requirements. While such flows financed over 40 per cent of the borrowing requirements of the non-oil developing countries in 1973, by 1981 this proportion had fallen to only 19.5 per cent.

As a result, the developing countries relied increasingly on net external borrowing to finance their growing resource gap. This category rose from only US $15.2 billion in 1973 to a peak of US $113 billion, or 79.1 per cent of gross borrowing requirements in 1981. The growth rate of total nominal debt of non-oil developing countries averaged approximately 20 per cent per annum during 1974 to 1981. Its acceleration meant that four times as much debt was accumulated during the 1970s as had been borrowed during the prior two decades. This rapid pace resulted in a dramatic increase in the stock of disbursed external debt, rising from US $130.1 billion at year-end 1973 to US $578 billion at year-end 1981 (see Table 1.2).

The growth of external debt was much more moderate when measured in real terms. Deflating the growth rate of external debt

Table 1.1 Balance of Payments Financing of Non-Oil Developing Countries, 1973–1984
(billion US dollars, or as indicated)

	1973	1974	1975	1976	1977	1978	1979	1980	1981	1982	1983	1984
I Balance of payments												
The sum of:												
Current account deficit	−11.3	−37.0	−46.3	−32.6	−29.6	−41.9	−62.1	−87.7	−108.3	−86.1	−52.1	−37.9
Asset transactions (a)	n.a.	n.a.	n.a.	n.a.	−5.1	−3.2	−6.6	−5.6	−14.3	−7.8	−8.5	−5.1
Recorded errors and omissions (b)	−3.8	−2.9	−5.6	−5.9	−6.4	−5.4	−0.9	−13.2	−16.5	−21.1	−9.6	−5.3
Use of reserves	−10.4	−2.7	1.6	−13.0	−11.2	−16.5	−11.7	−6.7	−3.7	4.1	−10.1	−19.1
equals:												
Gross borrowing requirement (c)	−25.5	−42.6	−50.3	−51.5	−52.3	−67.0	−81.3	−113.2	−142.8	−110.9	−80.3	−67.4
financed by:												
A. Non-debt-creating-flows	10.3	14.6	11.8	12.6	14.1	16.9	23.2	24.4	27.8	24.8	22.2	22.1
Foreign direct investment	4.2	5.3	5.3	5.0	5.3	7.2	9.5	9.5	13.5	12.0	9.1	8.6
Official transfers	5.5	8.7	7.1	7.5	8.3	8.3	11.7	12.4	13.3	12.9	12.8	13.0
Other flows (d)	0.6	0.6	−0.6	0.1	0.5	1.4	2.0	2.5	1.0	−0.1	0.3	0.5
B. Net external borrowing	15.2	28.0	38.5	38.9	36.6	49.6	57.7	88.0	113.0	79.5	55.8	44.4
Use of IMF credit	0.1	1.5	2.1	3.2	−0.2	−0.4	0.1	1.5	6.0	7.0	10.6	5.3
Other official sources	5.0	6.9	12.0	11.9	14.7	16.0	15.7	24.1	26.0	26.8	25.5	25.6
Long-term	4.9	6.8	11.7	10.5	12.7	14.6	17.0	22.2	25.1	25.7	26.7	25.8
Short-term	0.1	0.1	0.3	1.4	2.0	1.4	−1.3	1.9	0.9	1.1	−1.2	−0.2
Private sources	10.1	19.6	24.4	23.8	22.1	34.0	41.9	62.4	81.0	45.7	19.7	13.5
Long-term	6.8	11.3	15.4	17.5	11.7	26.3	35.7	35.7	58.7	32.1	38.3	22.9
Short-term	3.3	8.3	9.0	6.3	10.4	7.7	6.2	26.7	22.3	13.6	−18.6	−9.4
C. Arrears	0.0	0.0	0.0	0.0	1.6	0.5	0.4	0.8	2.0	6.6	2.3	0.9
II Share of gross borrowing requirements (%)												
a. current account deficit	44.3	86.9	92.0	63.3	56.6	62.5	76.4	77.5	75.8	77.6	64.9	56.2
b. capital flight	14.9	6.8	11.1	11.5	12.2	8.1	1.1	11.7	11.6	19.0	12.0	7.9
c. non-debt-creating flows	40.4	34.3	23.5	24.5	27.0	25.2	28.5	21.6	19.5	22.4	27.6	32.8
d. use of IMF credit	0.4	3.5	4.2	6.2	−0.4	−0.6	0.1	1.3	4.2	6.3	13.2	7.9
e. other official lending, net	19.6	16.2	23.9	23.1	28.1	23.9	19.3	21.3	18.2	24.2	31.8	38.0
f. private lending, net	39.6	46.0	48.5	46.2	42.3	50.7	51.5	55.1	56.7	41.2	24.5	20.0
g. arrears	0.0	0.0	0.0	0.0	3.1	0.7	0.5	0.7	1.4	6.0	2.9	1.3

Notes:

(a) Primarily trade credits granted by debtor country.

(b) Presumed to reflect primarily unrecorded capital outflow (i.e. capital flight).

(c) Understates actual gross borrowing requirements as it omits amortization which is included in net external borrowing.

(d) SDR allocations, valuation adjustments and gold monetization.

n.a. = not available

Sources: IMF, *World Economic Outlook*, 1983 and 1985 (Tables 25 and 41, respectively).

Table 1.2 External Debt of Non-Oil Developing Countries, 1973–1984(a)
(billion US dollars, or as indicated)

	1973	1974	1975	1976	1977	1978	1979	1980	1981	1982	1983	1984
I. *External debt*												
Total, nominal prices	130.1	160.8	190.8	228.0	291.3	342.6	406.3	489.5	578.3	655.2	693.5	730.5
Short-term	18.4	22.7	27.3	33.2	53.2	59.2	66.3	93.3	114.2	131.9	113.3	103.9
Medium-and long-term	111.7	138.1	163.5	194.8	238.1	283.4	340.0	396.2	464.1	523.3	580.2	626.6
Total, 1975 prices (b)	173.5	157.6	190.8	215.1	238.8	271.9	274.5	288.1	358.7	435.3	474.7	505.2
II. *Growth of debt (% change)*												
Total, nominal prices	—	23.6	18.7	19.5	27.8	17.6	18.6	20.5	18.1	13.3	5.8	5.3
Short-term	—	23.4	20.3	21.6	60.2	11.3	12.0	40.7	22.4	15.5	−14.1	−8.3
Medium and long-term	—	23.6	18.4	19.1	22.2	19.0	20.0	16.5	17.1	12.8	10.9	8.0
Total, 1975 prices (b)	—	−9.2	21.1	12.7	11.0	13.9	1.0	5.0	24.5	21.4	9.1	6.4
III. *Debt indicators (%)*												
Total debt/GDP	22.4	21.8	23.8	25.7	24.6	24.6	24.5	25.2	28.6	32.8	35.3	36.2
Total debt/exports (c)	115.4	104.6	122.4	125.5	131.6	131.6	121.4	115.1	128.0	150.8	158.2	152.3
Total debt/reserves (d)	320.0	370.0	470.0	430.0	430.0	400.0	430.0	510.0	590.0	710.0	690.0	640.0
Short-term debt/imports (months) (e)	2.3	1.8	2.1	2.4	3.2	3.0	2.6	2.8	3.3	4.2	3.8	3.3
Short-term debt/total debt	14.1	14.1	14.3	14.6	18.3	17.3	16.3	19.1	19.7	20.1	16.3	14.2

Notes:
(a) Excludes debt owed to the IMF.
(b) Deflated by the growth of export unit values for non-oil developing countries (1975 = 100).
(c) Exports of goods and services.
(d) Reserves are defined as all official foreign exchange holdings, Special Drawing Rights, and gold evaluated at SDR 35 per ounce.
(e) Imports of goods (fob) only.
Sources: IMF, *World Economic Outlook*, 1983 and 1985 (Tables 19, 30, 32, 33 and 37, 42, 47, 48, respectively).
IMF, *International Financial Statistics Yearbook*, 1981 and 1985.

with the growth of export unit values for the non-oil developing countries, the real increase was only 10 per cent per annum between 1974 and 1981. Moreover, given the the 5.1 per cent decline in export unit values in 1981, the debt's real growth in that year alone contributed over 30 per cent of its overall real increase between 1974 and 1981. Hence, over most of the 1970s, the growth of real debt recorded a fairly moderate rate of 7.9 per cent per annum.

Since credit-based import capacity for the developing countries advanced faster than their GDP, the level of total accumulated debt increased relative to nominal output. In 1973, the ratio of total external debt to GDP stood at 22.4 per cent for all non-oil developing countries. By 1981, it had increased to 28.6 per cent.

Between 1974 and 1980, the annual average growth of the value of external debt increased nearly 8 per cent faster than the growth of export prices for the non-oil developing country debtors. During the same period, the growth rate of export volume nearly matched this differential. Thus, the level of debt to exports in 1980 stood at virtually the same level as it had in 1973 (that is, 115 per cent), notwithstanding a peak in 1977 at 132 per cent. It was only in 1981, when the growth of export volume decelerated at the same time as the debtor's export prices began to fall, that the debt to export indicator increased sharply to 128 per cent.

The growth trend of short-term debt stayed broadly in line with that of medium and long-term debt during 1973 to 1976, so that its proportion of total debt remained between 14–15 per cent. During the years 1977–1981, the average growth rate of short-term debt rose, however, increasing its average proportion of total debt to 18 per cent. Although the amount of new short-term borrowings markedly increased after each of the oil price shocks of 1973 and 1979, these rates of borrowing were not excessive given the flow of merchandise imports. When short-term debt is measured as a percentage of merchandise imports, it remained at about 2.2 months during the period 1973–76, increasing to 2.9 months in the years 1977–80. Thus, since the trade finance facilities of the non-oil developing countries were underutilized before the second oil shock, the increase which brought short-term maturities in early 1981 to a level equivalent to a ninety–day financing of merchandise imports could not be considered excessive.

The Shift in Creditor Composition
The growth of lending during the 1970s was marked by a significant shift in creditor composition. Private creditors, particularly private commercial banks, displaced official creditors as the most important source of new borrowing by the non-oil developing countries. This shift resulted from a combination of funding constraints faced

by the official creditors and the abundant liquidity of the private capital markets.

The banks were awash with liquidity owing to the dramatic rise in OPEC financial deposits which had been channelled directly to commercial banks domiciled in their home developed countries and also to other offshore locations (for example, the Eurocurrency market). Owing to the synchronized recession of the industrial countries in 1975, the demand for new domestic credit was weak and these banks looked elsewhere for borrowers. Since the trade adjustment ability of industrial countries was much greater than the non-oil developing countries, they were able to limit the oil-price-induced current account deficit to only one year, 1974. Thus after 1974, the demand for foreign currency credit in these countries was much reduced, in contrast to the non-oil developing countries where trade adjustment was more difficult to achieve.

The other significant factor behind the shift in creditor composition was the inability of the official lending institutions such as the IMF, the International Bank for Reconstruction and Development (IBRD) and the bilateral credit agencies to adjust quickly to rapidly increasing borrowing needs. Johannes Witteveen, the former managing director of the IMF, has stated that the growth of IMF resources did not keep pace with the rising value of world trade during the 1970s (Heertje et al., 1984). Bilateral lending and official aid flows also failed to increase in line with world trade and the borrowing requirements of the non-oil developing countries.

As seen in Table 1.3, 46 per cent of the medium and long-term debt owed by the non-oil developing countries was supplied by official creditors in 1973.[7] By 1982, this share had dropped to only 38 per cent. This decline is understated since the majority of new short-term lending (not included in these numbers) was supplied primarily by private creditors. This increased 'privatization' of international financial intermediation during the 1970s led to further changes in the character of international lending.

The larger role of the private commercial banks meant that perceived creditworthiness rather than general development assistance or resource transfer became the predominant loan criterion. As a result, a tiered or segmented international loan market developed during the 1970s, with low income developing countries accumulating a declining proportion of the growing developing country debt. For example, while low income African debtors possessed 18 per cent and low income Asian countries held 15 per cent of the total disbursed debt in 1973, their respective shares had fallen to only 4 per cent and 7 per cent by 1982 (IBRD, 1984). Conversely, the net oil exporters and the middle and upper-income developing countries attracted a growing share of private credit.

Table 1.3 Medium and Long-Term External Debt of Non-Oil Developing Countries: Creditor Composition, 1973–1984 (billion US dollars, or percent)

	1973	1974	1975	1976	1977	1978	1979	1980	1981	1982	1983	1984
I. External debt												
Total medium and long-term (a)	111.8	138.1	163.5	194.9	238.1	283.1	340.0	396.2	464.1	523.2	580.2	626.6
Official creditor	51.0	60.2	68.4	80.2	100.0	118.8	136.2	157.7	176.8	198.4	220.8	241.4
Private creditor	60.8	77.9	95.1	114.7	138.1	164.3	203.8	238.5	287.3	324.8	359.4	385.2
Financial institution (b)	17.3	25.6	36.7	49.0	60.8	79.7	106.1	126.3	152.0	175.5	215.5	238.2
Other private	43.5	52.3	58.4	65.7	77.3	84.6	97.7	112.2	135.3	149.3	143.9	147.0
II. External debt												
Total medium and long-term (a)	100.0	100.0	100.0	100.0	100.0	100.0	100.0	100.0	100.0	100.0	100.0	100.0
Official creditor	45.6	43.6	41.8	41.1	42.0	42.0	40.1	39.8	38.1	37.9	38.1	38.5
Private creditor	54.4	56.4	58.2	58.9	58.0	58.0	59.9	60.2	61.9	62.1	61.9	61.5
Financial institution (b)	15.5	18.5	22.4	25.1	25.5	28.2	31.2	31.9	32.8	33.5	37.1	38.0
Other private	38.9	37.9	35.7	33.7	32.5	29.9	28.7	28.3	29.2	28.5	24.8	23.5

Notes:
(a) Excludes debt owed to the IMF.
(b) Includes only debt which has been guaranteed by an official agency of the debtor country.
Sources: IMF, *World Economic Outlook*, 1983 and 1985 (Tables 32 and 47, respectively).

The 'privatization' of international lending during the 1970s also led to an increase in the average borrowing terms. The average maturity structure of debt was shortened by extending new loans with a shorter maturity and grace period. At the same time, the average price of credit also rose.

The Rising Debt Service Burden

As seen in Table 1.4, the average amortization ratio (defined as the ratio of annual medium and long-term principal repayments to total medium and long-term debt) rose from 9.8 per cent in 1973 to 11.2 per cent in 1979 for non-oil developing countries. Thus, the average tenor of outstanding debt fell from 10.1 years to 8.9 years during this period. In an attempt to minimize risk in an uncertain market, the commercial banks rarely loaned money to developing country borrowers for more than eight to nine years. From 1973 to 1982, the average maturity of developing country debt, which originated from private sources and was guaranteed by an agency of the debtor country, stood at nine years. This was considerably shorter than the twenty-four year average for external debt originating from official creditors (IBRD, 1984). Similarly, the average private creditors' grace period (the time before principal repayment began) was only 3.5 years, while the equivalent period granted by official creditors was 6.4 years.

Many international bankers also thought that short-term loans (defined as liabilities with less than a one-year maturity) represented less risk than medium and long-term credits in an uncertain environment. This perception was one of the reasons underlying the rapid rise in short-term debt after the second oil shock in 1979. The shorter average maturity and grace period of long-term loans, combined with the rising proportion of short-term debt, meant that debt service payments increased sharply.

These trends also increased the roll-over burden or refinancing requirements of the debtor countries. For total developing country debt guaranteed by an agency of the debtor country, the roll-over ratio (debt-service to disbursements) averaged 49 per cent from 1973 to 1978 and rose to 72 per cent during 1979–1982 (IBRD, 1984). A higher roll-over ratio for a given capital inflow increases the debtor's exposure to a liquidity crisis by reducing the net financial transfer. This deterioration implied a rapidly rising dependence on new credit flows simply to roll-over existing principal payments.

The average interest rate paid by non-oil developing countries also increased due to the rising proportion of total debt supplied by private creditors. As shown in Table 1.4, it rose from 5.3 per cent in 1973 to a peak of 9.8 per cent in 1982. Since commercial bank loan rates were not subsidized they stood well above average official

Table 1.4 External Borrowing Terms for Non-Oil Developing Countries, 1973–1984.
(billion US dollars, or percent)

	1973	1974	1975	1976	1977	1978	1979	1980	1981	1982	1983	1984
I. *Debt service payments*												
Total, excluding short-term amortization	18.0	22.1	25.1	27.7	35.6	50.2	65.6	76.1	98.5	109.5	95.1	103.2
Interest payments (a)	6.9	9.3	10.5	10.9	13.7	19.0	27.4	39.1	56.0	64.3	59.2	60.9
Amortization payments (b)	11.1	12.8	14.6	16.8	21.9	31.2	38.2	37.0	42.5	45.2	35.9	42.3
Total, including short-term amortization	36.3	44.8	52.4	61.0	88.8	109.7	131.9	169.4	212.7	241.4	208.4	207.1
Total, 1975 prices (c)	48.4	43.9	52.4	57.5	72.8	87.1	89.1	98.6	127.0	153.2	136.1	135.4
Net financial transfer (d)	8.3	18.7	27.9	27.5	22.9	30.6	30.3	48.9	57.0	15.3	-3.4	-16.5
II. *Debt service indicators* (%)												
Debt service ratio, excluding short-term amortization	15.9	14.4	16.1	15.3	16.1	19.3	19.6	17.9	21.8	25.2	21.7	21.5
Interest payments ratio (e)	6.1	6.1	6.7	6.0	6.2	7.3	8.2	9.2	12.4	14.8	13.5	12.7
Amortization payments ratio (e)	9.8	8.3	9.4	9.3	9.9	12.0	11.4	8.7	9.4	10.4	8.2	8.8
Average interest rate (f)	5.3	5.8	5.5	4.9	4.7	5.5	6.7	8.0	9.7	9.8	8.5	8.3
Average amortization rate (g)	9.9	9.3	8.9	8.6	9.2	11.0	11.2	9.3	9.2	8.6	6.2	6.8
Total debt service ratio (e)	149.5	198.3	208.3	242.0	309.9	369.8	466.6	594.5	664.5	675.9	646.6	687.1
Net transfer/imports (fob)	8.7	12.4	17.6	16.5	11.6	13.0	9.9	12.3	13.6	4.1	-1.0	-4.4
LIBOR (annual average) (h)	9.3	11.2	7.6	6.1	6.4	9.2	12.0	14.2	16.5	13.3	9.8	11.0

Notes

(a) Includes interest payments on total disbursed external liabilities (including short-term debt).
(b) Includes principal repayments on medium and long-term debt only.
(c) Deflated by the growth of export unit values for non-oil developing countries (1975=100).
(d) Defined as the difference between gross loan disbursements and total debt service payments.
(e) Total payments as a percentage of exports of goods and services.
(f) Total interest payments as a percentage of total external debt.
(g) Medium and long-term principal repayments as a percentage of medium and long-term debt.
(e) Total debt service payments as a percentage of medium and long-term debt.
(h) The six-month US dollar deposit rate in London.

Sources: IMF, *World Economic Outlook*, 1983 and 1985 (Tables 25, 35 and 37, 41, 47, 49, respectively).
IMF, *International Financial Statistics Yearbook*, 1981 and 1985.

rates. The IBRD (1984) reports that during 1973 to 1982 the average interest rate charged by private creditors stood at 11.0 per cent. This compares to an average rate of 5.5 per cent charged by official creditors over the same period. The Development Assistance Committee Official Development Assistance loan rates and export credit rates were even lower, averaging only 4.9 per cent from 1972–1982 (OECD, 1982). As a result of the higher interest rates charged by private creditors, the IBRD (1984) reported that only 48 per cent of the debt in 1981 generated a full 78 per cent of the total interest cost.

Not only did private creditors charge higher fixed rates but they also relied increasingly upon floating-rate debt. The cost of funds to commercial banks became more volatile and expensive due to higher inflation rates and tighter monetary policy in key OECD countries. As a result of financial reform, the advent of floating rate debt shifted the immediate cost of this uncertainty from the lender to the borrower. Of the developing country debt which was guaranteed by an agency of the debtor, the proportion of floating rate debt increased from only 12 per cent in 1973 to 38 per cent in 1982 (IBRD, 1984). This increase is probably understated since much of the unguaranteed medium and long-term commercial bank debt, (not included in these totals) would have been priced with floating rates. Moreover, since short-term debt could be re-priced when it was rolled over, its growing proportion also effectively raised the floating rate component of total debt.

1.4 Systemic Rigidities in International Financial Intermediation

By the end of 1980, the international financial markets, and the accumulated level of developing country debt in particular, were characterized by certain rigidities which weakened the stability of international financial intermediation.

The inability and unwillingness of non-oil developing countries to implement adequate balance of payment adjustment programmes meant that their gross borrowing requirements increased every year from 1973 to 1981. This trend, combined with the inadequate growth of non-debt-creating flows, resulted in the excessively rapid growth of external debt. It could be argued, however, that the borrowers were simply responding to market signals. For example, the real interest cost of external borrowing, when deflated by the growth of developing country export prices, was negative throughout most of the 1970s. Therefore, the perceived real cost of accumulating external liabilities and the incentive to implement trade adjustment policies were both minimal. Moreover, these trends created expectations that negative borrowing costs would indefinitely continue. Hence, the abundance of cheap credit reduced the incentives for trade adjustment and created a propensity to overborrow. Thus, debt grew more quickly than either output or export revenue.

The rapidly rising debt level, combined with a shorter average maturity structure, resulted in rising amortization payments (see Table 1.4). The growth of principal repayments also advanced more quickly than total export receipts. While this ratio averaged 9.3 per cent per annum during the period 1973–1977, it increased to an annual average of 10.7 percent from the years 1978–1980. The proportion of interest payments to export receipts also rose during this period. Averaging only 6.2 per cent per annum during the period 1973–1977, interest payments consumed an annual average of 8.2 per cent of export receipts from 1978 to 1980. These trends meant that debt service payments were consuming a larger proportion of export revenue.

Table 1.4 on p. 16 shows that the debt service ratio for all non-oil developing countries increased from 15.9 per cent in 1973 to 21.8 per cent in 1981. Since debt service payments were growing more quickly than the external debt itself, the roll-over ratio also was increasing. Thus, larger gross borrowings were required to maintain a given net financial transfer. Such a trend was clearly unsustainable. Although the outstanding external debt increased every year from 1973 to 1982, the net financial transfer increased only six of those ten years. Moreover, the ratio of the net financial transfer to merchandise imports peaked in 1975. Despite a continual increase in external debt, the credit-based import capacity of developing countries declined from 1976 to 1979. Finally in 1980 and 1981, when the net financial transfer accelerated markedly, the credit-based import capacity improved. Even though the net financial transfer was over twice as high in 1981 as it had been in 1975, it could finance only 78 per cent of the 1975 import bill, since debt service payments had risen by almost fourfold over this time period. This rising dependence on the flow of new credit simply to service external debt payments increased the vulnerability of the debtors to the cessation of new lending (that is, a liquidity crisis).

While the debtor countries accumulated foreign exchange reserves during most years in the 1970s, the growth rate of these international assets did not keep pace with rising import requirements. The ratio of international reserves to import expenditures declined from an adequate 3.8 months of import cover in 1973 to only 2.0 months in 1981. This trend restricted financial manoeuverability. For example, this reduction made it less likely that external economic shocks could be buffered by reserve usage, thus limiting the time for adequate trade adjustment policies to be implemented.

Besides these borrowing mistakes by the debtor countries, there were also aspects of lending behaviour which created rigidities in the financial system. Whether due to a consensus assessment of low-risk borrowers or to the 'herd' behaviour of lending, there developed an extreme concentration of private commercial bank lending to a very small group of countries. Table 1.5 shows that in 1981 the disbursed external debt of the top five developing country debtors represented over 36 per cent of total BIS-bank claims outside the reporting area. As a share of BIS claims to developing countries only, the debt of the top five debtors represented an even greater proportion (that is, 55.2 per cent). No matter how sanguine the assessment for these countries had been, such extreme concentration was ill advised.

Since the five largest developing country debtors (Argentina, Brazil, Mexico, South Korea and Venezuela) relied most heavily on commercial bank credit, these countries also accumulated the majority of the floating-rate debt. By assuming the risk of interest rate fluctuations, these large international borrowers increased their vulnerability to ex post increases in the interest cost of 'old' debt. Given that several rules for prudent borrowing are a function of the interest cost of external debt, such uncertainty is unacceptable. Variable interest rate debt increases the exogeneity of a country's rescheduling probability and thus greatly complicates the planning process.

Argy (1981) has noted that although the Eurobanks 'did not engage in any significant maturity transformation in 1971 or 1974, . . . the situation had changed significantly [by 1977].'[8] He continues, 'In May, 1977 the liabilities maturing in three months or less amounted to 66% of total Euro-bank liabilities while their assets maturing in three months or less represented only 53% of their assets. At the same time, while some 7% of their liabilities matured in a year or longer, 24% of their assets fell in this category.' This trend posed two problems for international lending.

First, maturity transformation tended to increase liquidity in the global capital markets which, in turn, exerted downward pressure on lending spreads and interest rates. The average spread on new publicized medium and long-term international bank credit commitments to developing countries fell progressively from approximately 1.5 per cent in 1975 to below 1 per cent in 1979 (IMF, 1985b). The lower cost of borrowing increased the proclivity to overborrow. Secondly, maturity transformation made the Euro-banks more vulnerable to a liquidity squeeze if their depositors (for

Table 1.5 Geographic Composition of Industrial Country Banks' Exposure, 1976–1984
(billion US dollars, or percent)

	1976	1977	1978	1979	1980	1981	1982	1983	1984
I Total BIS-bank claims (a)	160.6	217.0	298.3	366.1	426.2	489.0	531.2	560.8	569.6
of which:									
a. Other developed countries	42.8	52.7	64.7	74.4	87.0	101.6	116.0	128.4	137.6
b. Eastern Europe	25.5	36.6	47.6	56.1	59.7	60.7	53.3	50.3	46.7
c. Developing countries	92.3	127.7	186.0	235.6	279.5	326.7	361.9	382.1	385.3
of which:									
Latin America	57.7	74.5	97.1	131.3	162.9	196.6	214.2	225.2	227.3
Middle East	10.6	18.1	34.4	33.7	34.1	36.3	40.8	40.1	39.3
Africa	6.9	12.5	23.1	28.7	30.9	32.7	35.2	35.4	33.7
Asia	17.1	22.6	31.4	41.9	51.6	61.1	71.7	81.4	85.0
Note: five major LDC debtors (b)	50.3	64.5	84.7	115.7	149.1	180.5	199.8	210.5	214.2
II Share of BIS claims (%)									
a. Other developed countries	26.7	24.3	21.7	20.3	20.4	20.8	21.8	22.9	24.2
b. Eastern Europe	15.9	16.9	16.0	15.3	14.0	12.4	10.0	9.0	8.2
c. Latin America	35.9	34.3	32.6	35.9	38.2	40.2	40.3	40.2	39.9
d. Middle East	6.6	8.3	11.5	9.2	8.0	7.4	7.7	7.2	6.9
e. Africa	4.3	5.8	7.7	7.8	7.3	6.7	6.6	6.3	5.9
f. Asia	10.6	10.4	10.5	11.4	12.1	12.5	13.5	14.5	14.9
g. Top five LDC debtors	31.3	29.7	28.4	31.6	35.0	36.9	37.6	37.5	37.6

Notes:
(a) Represents gross cross-border loan exposure outside reporting area for BIS-reporting banks in the Group of Ten, Luxembourg, Austria, Denmark, Finland, Ireland, Norway, Spain, Bahamas, Bahrain, Cayman Islands, Hong Kong, Netherlands Antilles, Singapore and US banks in Panama.

(b) Argentina, Brazil, South Korea, Mexico and Venezuela.
Sources: Bank for International Settlements, 'The Maturity Distribution of International Bank Lending', various issues.

example, OPEC) decided to make large net withdrawals. In such an event, the banks would be less likely to roll-over existing long-term loans or grant new long-term loans.

By the end of 1980 or early in 1981, these rigidities in the international capital markets revealed the unsustainability of the growth of developing country debt. In contrast, the professional consensus was that the level of developing country external debt was not excessively high and that these capital inflows had been constructively utilized.[9] Gross fixed investment as a proportion of GDP had risen concurrently with the rapid accumulation of external liabilities. This, it was argued, provided for the long-term creditworthiness of the debtor countries.[10] The natural resource endowment and the export performance of certain large debtors was cited as additional proof of sustained creditworthiness. This optimistic professional consensus and the continued aggressive lending behaviour of the international commercial banks in 1981 belied the true instability of the international recycling process at that time.

The intensification of a series of economic and financial disturbances in 1981 severely impacted the debtor countries and resulted in a debt payment crisis of unequalled proportions. A viable long-term solution to this crisis has yet to be found.

End-Chapter Notes

1 Representative examples of the growth-cum-indebtedness literature include King, 1968; Feder, 1978; and Erbe, 1982; all of which assume the savings-investment gap to be binding. Refer to Feder, 1981 for a model in which the foreign exchange gap is assumed to be the relevant constraint. For two-gap models which attempt to quantify aid policy decisions, please see Chenery and MacEwan, 1966 and Chenery and Strout, 1966. Alternative views to this prevailing orthodoxy have proliferated over the past decade. See Amin, 1976; Emmanuel, 1972; and Payer, 1974 for examples of this alternative viewpoint.

2 The US Interest Equalization Tax of 1963, the Voluntary Foreign Credit Constraints of 1965 (which became mandatory in 1968), and the Office of Foreign Direct Investment Guidelines of 1965 are examples of the legislative effort to improve the capital account of the US balance of payments. These laws and guidelines restricted the ability of foreign companies to source debt instruments in the US capital market and also required US multinationals to seek funding abroad for their overseas operations. Thus, these actions increased the demand for alternative sources of credit outside of the United States.

3 Freedman, 1977 has stated that the impetus to the growth of the Euro-dollar market during the 1960s can be interpreted as being primarily

demand-led (an outward shift in the demand curve), while the growth in the 1970s was supply-led. Although both growth patterns will increase the size of the market, he argues that the demand-led growth will raise the deposit and loan rates in the Euromarket relative to the domestic markets, while the supply-led growth pattern will lower them vis-à-vis the domestic market. This structural shift in the Euromarket's growth pattern may have increased the proclivity for global debtors to over borrow in the 1970s, since the excess liquidity tended to lower the interest rates, depress the spreads, and reduce borrowing costs.

4 By 1975, the banking systems in most developed countries were flush with liquidity and faced weak demand from their traditional wholesale and retail customers due to the synchronized OECD recession. Thus, untypical borrowers such as Eastern Europe and the developing countries became the outlet for much of these funds. Since many banks which participated in this lending were unfamiliar with these new international customers and with the new types of risk which they embodied, credit analysis in some cases may have been inadequate. Pressure to maintain rates of profit by accumulating new assets within this uncertain environment may have meant that asset growth rather than asset quality took precedence. Kindleberger, 1981 has argued that many past episodes of foreign lending can be characterized by a 'euphoric stage' where the 'promoters are to blame as much as the wildly optimistic and often profligate borrowers' for the rapid growth of debt. In such cases excessively rapid debt growth is followed by a period of lending 'revulsion' and, typically, loan default.

5 According to the UNCTAD (1985), more than 33 per cent of the developing country exports by value are subject to measures in developed countries which constrain the growth of export volumes. Moreover, of the commodities in which it is generally acknowledged that the developing countries currently hold a comparative advantage, the impact of these trade restrictions falls disproportionately on the developing countries. For example, while 65 per cent of these products exported from developing countries were subject to non-tariff barriers (NTBs) in developed country markets, only 23 per cent of the same product groups exported by other developed countries were subject to NTBs. It is also apparent that NTBs are increasing over time. UNCTAD (1985) has reported that such measures as countervailing duties and anti-dumping actions in the developed market economy countries have increased from 124 instances in 1979 to 405 in 1984. In addition, most of these measures have been directed at the largest debtor countries. Among the 405 trade restrictions levelled against the developing countries, nearly 70 per cent were directed at Brazil, South Korea, Mexico, and Taiwan Province of China, which includes three of the five largest developing country debtors.

6 Amortization payments are omitted from the gross borrowing requirements as they have been included in net external borrowing. Hence, actual gross borrowing requirements are understated and the proportion of contributing liability flows are somewhat overstated.

7 Earlier in the decade, the proportion of developing country debt owed to official creditors was even greater. The World Bank, 1981 reports that loans from official sources constituted 54 per cent of outstanding debt at the end of 1971.

8 Maturity transformation is defined as the degree to which a bank's asset or loan maturity structure differs from the maturity structure of its liabilities or deposits. If the average maturity structure of the former is significantly longer than that of the latter, then a bank is subject to liquidity risk.

9 For examples of this viewpoint, refer to Solomon, 1977 and 1981 and Sachs, 1982a.

10 Increased investment is merely a necessary, not a sufficient condition for long-term creditworthiness or solvency. Other important criteria for investment planning and sustained solvency include the new investment's rate of return vis-à-vis the cost of external funding, its sectoral composition amongst tradable versus non-tradable goods, and the resulting shift of the domestic and reciprocal offer curves.

2.
The International Debt Crisis, 1982 to the Present

2.1 Introduction

The relatively smooth global recycling process during most of the 1970s was the result of the extensive international capital market combined with low commercial bank exposure to the developing countries. Despite a continual increase in the borrowing requirements of the non-oil developing countries during this time, the growth of private bank lending was able to meet the majority of these needs. By the late 1970s, however, the cost of servicing the debt was accelerating due to the rising proportion of floating interest rate debt and due to the shortened maturity structure of overall debt. With the non-debt related borrowing requirements of the developing countries also increasing yearly, the growth of gross loan disbursements had to accelerate to produce a greater net financial transfer. Hence, by the early 1980s the large level of developing country debt combined with the rising debt cost meant that the capital flow requirements were becoming excessively large and unsustainable.

A new series of economic shocks to the global trade and financial markets in general and to the developing country debtors in particular began in 1979 and intensified in 1981. These disturbances exacerbated the dependence of non-oil developing countries on external private financial flows.

The ability of the debtor countries to adjust to these exogenous shocks was limited, in part, by their economic policy errors committed during the years of international borrowing with negative interest rates. Certain debtor country economic policy errors continued into the 1980s. The policy response of key developed countries also constrained the ability of the debtor countries to make adjustments. Once the crisis occurred, further policy mistakes and an unwillingness on the part of some debtors to implement adequate stabilization programmes also hindered effective adjustment.

With growing signs of deteriorating sovereign balance sheets due to unabated borrowing requirements, rising debt and debt service levels, falling import cover and growing payment arrears, the perceived creditworthiness of developing countries fell. Thus by 1982, the ability and willingness of private international banks to continue lending at the pace of the prior nine years also declined.

The nature and magnitude of the exogenous economic disturbances (which were exacerbated by the policies of key industrial countries), combined with the accumulated policy errors of the debtor countries and the inability and unwillingness of the international banks to continue to lend ever increasing amounts of new money, ultimately made the recycling process untenable. In 1980 the growth of payment arrears began to accelerate and the incidence of requests for debt rescheduling increased as a means of dealing with the ever-growing imbalance between developing country resources and requirements. By the end of 1981, it was apparent that the debt crisis had begun in the centrally planned economies of Eastern Europe. In 1982, the fears of all concerned parties were confirmed when the payments crisis became generalized, spreading to the market economies of the non-oil developing countries.

2.2 External Shocks to the Debtor Countries

The OPEC Oil-Price Shock of 1979–80
The primary effect of the 1979–80 OPEC oil-price shock was a large fall in the terms of trade of the developing countries in 1980. As can be seen in Table 2.1, when the price of oil rose by 35.9 per cent in 1979 and by 66.1 per cent in 1980, the terms of trade of the non-oil developing countries fell by 1.9 per cent and 5.7 per cent, respectively. This decline resulted in a significant erosion of income and, hence, larger borrowing requirements for the non-oil developing countries. As a result, the net financial transfer to the non-oil developing countries increased from US $30.3 billion in 1979 to US $48.9 billion in 1980 and US $57 billion in 1981.

The impact of the OPEC price increase also meant a net income loss to the industrialized countries due to a deterioration in their terms of trade. However, unlike the period after the first oil shock, the policy response of key developed countries was motivated more by a fear of accelerating inflation than by a concern about rising unemployment.

Industrial Country Policies and Performance
The wage-price spiral after the first oil shock led to inflation which was persistently high by historical standards. Moreover, the second oil shock dramatically increased the wholesale price index of the

Table 2.1 External Economic Shocks to Non-Oil Developing Countries, 1973–1984 (percent change, or as indicated)

	1973–1977(f)	1978	1979	1980	1981	1982	1983	1984
Industrial country factors								
Real GNP growth	3.0	4.1	3.5	1.3	1.6	-0.2	2.6	4.9
Wholesale price index	10.9	5.6	9.7	13.4	8.7	5.3	3.2	4.4
Broad Money velocity	-0.3	0.6	1.0	2.0	1.5	-2.1	-3.3	0.6
Real federal funds rate (%)(a)	-0.6	-0.3	-0.1	-0.1	6.0	6.1	5.8	5.9
Income elasticity of non-oil import demand (b)	2.1	2.3	3.0	1.8	0.3	-16.1	2.8	3.6
Net financial transfer to developing countries ($ bill.)(c)	21.1	30.6	30.3	48.9	57.0	15.3	-3.4	-16.5
Price disturbances								
Oil price (average $ per barrel)(d)	9.4	12.7	17.3	28.7	32.5	33.5	29.3	28.5
Oil price	65.7	2.3	35.9	66.1	13.4	3.0	-12.5	-2.9
Six-month LIBOR (average %)	8.1	9.2	12.0	14.2	16.5	13.3	9.8	11.0
Real six-month LIBOR (e)	-9.3	5.4	-4.6	-0.6	21.6	19.9	12.7	11.1
Terms of trade	0.6	-5.3	-1.9	-5.7	-8.0	-3.3	-0.1	4.6
SDR/US dollar rate (average)	-1.0	-6.7	-3.1	-0.7	10.4	6.8	3.3	4.3

Notes:
(a) US rate deflated by average annual CPI rate.
(b) Ratio of growth in non-oil imports to growth of GNP.
(c) Gross loan disbursements from private and multilateral sources, less total debt service payments.
(d) Average annual price in US dollars of Saudi Arabian (Ras Tanura).
(e) Deflated by the growth of export unit values for non-oil developing countries (1975=100).
(f) Annual arithmetic average.

Sources: IMF, *World Economic Outlook*, 1983 and 1985 (Tables 1, 10, 25 and 2, 20, 27, 41, respectively).
IMF, *International Financial Statistics Yearbook*, 1981, 1985, and January 1986.

industrial countries from 5.6 per cent in 1978 to 9.7 per cent in 1979 and further to 13.4 per cent in 1980. As shown in Table 2.1 on p. 26, the growth of broad money velocity in the industrialized countries concurrently accelerated from 0.6 in 1978 to 2.0 in 1980, showing signs that inflationary expectations were increasing rapidly. At that time, there was growing evidence that these changes in expectations were skewing resource allocation away from productive investment toward precious metals, real estate, and other unproductive tangible assets. Thus, in the United States in particular, a tight monetary policy was implemented starting in late 1979.

The pursuit of tight monetary policy in the United States immediately increased nominal interest rates both at home and abroad as reflected by the jump in the six-month London Inter-Bank Offer Rate (LIBOR) rate from an average of 9.2 per cent in 1978 to 12.0 per cent in 1979 and 14.2 per cent in 1980. However, real interest rates faced by the non-oil developing countries remained negative due to the acceleration of their export price increases.

By late 1980 there were initial signs that tight money was achieving its intended effect. GNP growth of the industrialized countries decelerated from an average rate of 3.5 per cent in 1979 to 1.3 per cent in 1980. The income elasticity of non-oil import demand also fell from 3.0 in 1979 to 1.8 in 1980. Since the 1980 recessions in the United States and the United Kingdom were not synchronized with those of other major OECD countries, slower average growth of the industrialized countries and a declining propensity to import non-oil merchandise did not have an immediate detrimental effect on the non-oil developing countries. Thus, the real growth of non-oil developing country exports actually accelerated in 1980.

The spread of the recession to other industrialized countries, combined with continued negative growth in the UK and a weak recovery in the United States, resulted in continued sluggish industrial country growth which advanced only 1.6 per cent in 1981. During the 1981 recession the OECD countries pursued policies of expenditure switching and expenditure reduction, since they had been foreign exchange constrained and were losing their international reserves. Thus, the short-term income elasticity of non-oil import demand of the industrialized countries became inelastic in 1981. This trend, coupled with weak OECD GNP growth, resulted in a further decline in the terms of trade and a slowdown in the growth of export volume for the non-oil developing countries. These trends worsened in 1982 when the United States experienced another recession which was now synchronized with those in other important 'locomotive' countries, such as the Federal Republic of Germany. The adjustment capabilities of the developing countries were further impaired by Japan, which, although avoiding a recession, allowed an undervalued currency to achieve ever larger current account surpluses. The extended OECD recession and their expenditure switching policies impaired the trade adjustment capability of the non-oil developing countries, thus precluding a reduction of the current account deficit of the latter from 1979 to 1981.

The tight money recession in the United States in 1980 and the continued high cost of credit after 1980 started to abate the growth of inflationary expectations.[1] The rate of price increases, both in the USA and other industrialized countries, decelerated in 1981. The growth of money velocity in the industrialized countries also decelerated in 1981 and became negative in 1982 as the initial recessions in the United States and United Kingdom were transmitted to other OECD countries. However, the continuation of tight money in the United States after 1980, combined with looser fiscal policy, meant that nominal interest rates stayed abnormally high. Thus, with the inflation rate decelerating, real interest rates, which had been negative virtually throughout the entire post–1973 period of international lending, became sharply positive.

This persistence of tight monetary policy in the United States from 1979 to 1982 worsened the debt crisis, not only by lengthening the OECD recession but also by transmitting three separate price shocks to the non-oil developing countries, namely, higher interest rates, a stronger US dollar, and declining terms of trade.

The magnitude of the real interest rate shock to the non-oil developing countries was even greater than the swing in the US real federal funds rate. While the real federal funds rate swung from an average rate of −0.1 per cent in 1980 to 6.0 per cent in 1981, the real six-month LIBOR rate jumped from −0.6 per cent to 21.6 per cent over the same period.[2] As can be seen in Table 2.1 on p. 26, these high real rates have persisted since 1981, although currently they have eased somewhat. This unexpected exogenous increase in the cost of servicing foreign debt was the primary reason that interest payments of the developing countries rose over 43 per cent from US $39.1 billion in 1980 to US $56 billion in 1981.

The rise in the value of the US dollar on a trade weighted basis represented another price shock to the indebted non-oil developing countries. Since the vast majority of international debt is denominated in US dollars, the rise in its value effectively raised the size of the external debt measured in terms of local currency, increasing the debtor's real resource pay-out burden. This increased cost would have been proportionate to the share of US-dollar-denominated debt in each country's total foreign debt. From Table 2.1 it is apparent that this shock continued from 1981 until February, 1985, with the largest annual increase of 10.4 per cent occurring in 1981.

The volatility of the US dollar also affected the value of trade flows. For many Asian countries, export receipts are more US dollar-denominated than import expenditures; the appreciating US dollar therefore produced a price-related windfall gain. In contrast, Latin American countries faced US $ receipts and payments which were more equally balanced and, hence, did not receive a windfall gain from the US $ appreciation. Since early 1985, the negative effect of a declining US $ on many Asian countries has meant lower export receipts (measured in domestic currency) and higher domestic resource import costs.

The Behaviour of Private Commercial Banks

When the second OPEC oil-price shock occurred in 1979–80 the loan exposure of the international banks to developing countries was extremely high, unlike the situation which existed immediately after the first oil shock in 1973–74. This is particularly true when the loan exposure is measured as a proportion of the banks' capital. Although the rate of new lending accelerated in 1980 and 1981, the private banks could not sustain such rates given gross exposure levels. As shown in Table 2.2, the loans of US banks to all developing countries equalled 144.9 per cent of bank capital in 1978. By 1981, however, total loan exposure vis-à-vis capital rose to 191.7 per cent, with this exposure concentrated in the large money centre banks. While the banking industry's overall exposure represented 183.3 per cent of capital in 1982, the claims of the nine largest banks on the developing countries stood at 284 per cent. Federally regulated legal lending limits for US bank exposure to individual countries also became a constraint by the early 1980s. Thus, the ability of the private banking industry to supply the developing countries' continually rising borrowing needs was increasingly limited.

With the confluence of many of these external shocks during 1981, it was apparent that the recycling process was becoming unsustainable due to the rapidly deteriorating creditworthiness of the non-oil developing countries. Thus in 1982, the growth of net new lending of the private banks sharply decelerated. From a peak of 23.1 per cent in 1981, the growth of US bank lending decelerated to only 3.5 per cent by 1983. While net external lending to non-oil developing countries had been US $81 billion in 1981, this flow fell to US $45.7 billion in 1982. This decline in net new lending, coupled with the increase in interest payments, meant that the net financial transfer fell even more precipitously from US $57 billion to just US $15.3 billion in 1982. Undisbursed commitments as a proportion of total bank debt also declined from 33 per cent in 1978 to just 12 per cent in 1983 (IMF, 1985b).

Table 2.2   Risks and Lending Behaviour of US Banks, 1977–1983
(percentage, or as indicated)

I Lending exposure of US banks to developing countries relative to total bank capital (a)	*1977*	*1978*	*1979*	*1980*	*1981*	*1982*	*1983*
A. All US banks to:							
Developing countries (b)	150.7	144.9	159.4	169.2	191.7	183.3	165.9
Non OPEC developing countries	119.1	114.7	124.3	132.3	154.9	146.0	134.7
Top five debtors (c)	100.2	81.3	88.6	98.7	112.3	111.0	99.8
Five next largest debtors (d)	20.0	20.1	23.0	25.1	29.3	28.6	30.3
B. Nine largest US banks to:							
Developing countries (b)	n.a.	n.a.	n.a.	n.a.	n.a.	284.0	263.4
Non OPEC developing countries	163.0	167.0	182.0	200.0	230.0	221.0	209.0
Top five debtors (c)	n.a.	n.a.	n.a.	n.a.	n.a.	165.1	150.6
Five next largest debtors (d)	n.a.	n.a.	n.a.	n.a.	n.a.	45.0	41.7
C. 15 next largest US banks to:							
Developing countries (b)	n.a.	n.a.	n.a.	n.a.	n.a.	189.6	179.9
Non OPEC developing countries	106.0	110.0	112.0	125.0	151.0	150.0	145.0
Top five debtors (c)	n.a.	n.a.	n.a.	n.a.	n.a.	117.8	114.6
Five next largest debtors (d)	n.a.	n.a.	n.a.	n.a.	n.a.	29.3	25.8
II Debtor performance and bank lending behaviour							
Non-oil LDC arrears (US$ billion)	1.6	0.5	0.4	0.8	2.0	6.6	2.3
Growth of US bank lending (%)	11.3	18.4	18.4	22.0	23.1	11.2	3.5
Undisbursed commitments to total US bank claims (%)	n.a.	33.0	23.0	22.0	18.0	13.0	12.0

Notes:
  (a) Exposure includes all cross-border and non-local currency lending.
  (b) Excludes offshore banking centres, including Barbados, Bermuda, Cayman Islands, Hong Kong, Lebanon, Liberia, Netherlands Antilles, Panama and Singapore.
  (c) Argentina, Brazil, Republic of Korea, Mexico and Venezuela.
  (d) Chile, Colombia, Indonesia, Peru, and the Philippines.
Sources: Federal Financial Institution Examination Council, Country Exposure Lending Survey.
  H.S. Terrel, 'Bank lending to developing countries: recent developments and some considerations for the future', in *Federal Reserve Bulletin*, October, 1984.
  IMF, Recent Developments in External Debt Rescheduling, October, 1985 (Table 5).
  UNCTAD, *Trade and Development Report*, 1985 (Table 21).

Credit-based import capacity of the non-oil developing countries fell accordingly, with import volume dropping 7.5 per cent in 1982. Since this expenditure reduction comprised both non-compressible (or essential) imports and compressible (or non-essential) items, the credit restriction resulted in an externally induced growth slow down in the non-oil developing countries. The dramatic restriction in access to credit meant that it was no longer possible to obtain enough new financing to roll over amortization payments and fund current import expenditures. By drastically reducing new lending, the international banking industry generally, and the small US regional banks in particular, worsened the liquidity of the debtor countries and contributed to the increased incidence of debt payment arrears.

Problems of illiquidity can be rectified fairly quickly. It is likely, however, that many of the debt reschedulings which occurred in the 1980s reflected a condition of insolvency. While the persistence of some of the external shocks outlined in this section have resulted in this long-term debt servicing problem, accumulated economic policy errors on the part of the debtor countries themselves also significantly contributed to this condition.

2.3 Economic Policy Choices of the Debtor Countries

Development Policy
One of the fundamental mistakes made by the non-oil developing countries during the post–1973 period was to attempt to achieve growth targets which were too ambitious. Although there are many pressures in a developing country which bias the development plan toward rapid growth of output, such targets should be tempered to ensure their sustainability, particularly given the likelihood of external shocks. Hence, a prudent growth target should reflect the availability of domestic resources such as savings, raw materials, manpower, intermediate goods and capital equipment, plus the utilization of a reasonable margin (for example, 2–3 per cent of GDP) of foreign resources. The long-term growth of demand should be planned and managed to match the growth trend of this domestic and foreign resource supply.

As shown in Table 2.3, the growth of GDP for the non-oil developing countries averaged 5.4 per cent from 1973 to 1981. This average rate of GDP growth, although matching that in the period from 1961 to 1972, was excessively high due to the deteriorating external economic environment. For example, while the terms of trade for this group of countries was virtually unchanged from 1961 to 1972, the growth of import prices exceeded the growth of export prices by 22.4 per cent from 1973 to 1981 (IMF, 1985a). Thus, the effective income loss from this terms of trade decline meant that an increased reliance on foreign resources and external debt accumulation was required to sustain the same average rate of GDP growth.

Aggressive investment programmes are typically a major component of rapid GDP growth in developing countries. The average ratio of investment to GDP for the non-oil developing countries stood at 24.8 per cent during the period 1973–1977 and rose to an average ratio of 25.5 per cent from 1978 to 1981. This rate of gross fixed capital formation was too high, and its acceleration through the second oil shock (especially given the resulting terms-of-trade income loss) was unwarranted for several reasons.

Table 2.3 Economic Policy Stance of Non-Oil Developing Countries, 1973–1984
(percent change, or as indicated)

	1973–1977(h)	1978	1979	1980	1981	1982	1983	1984
I. *Development policy*								
Real growth of GDP	5.4	6.3	5.1	4.6	3.4	2.2	1.9	4.2
Investment/GDP (%)	24.8	25.4	25.7	25.8	25.2	22.6	22.6	23.3
ICOR(a)	4.6	4.0	5.0	5.6	7.4	10.6	11.9	5.4
Savings/GDP (%)(b)	21.6	22.5	22.1	21.5	20.2	19.0	n.a.	n.a.
II. *Trade adjustment policy*								
Current account/exports, G & S (%)	−18.9	−16.1	−18.6	−20.6	−24.0	−19.8	−11.9	−7.9
Export volume	16.2	9.5	8.4	8.7	7.6	1.8	5.9	11.3
Import volume	16.0	8.6	10.2	7.2	2.7	−7.5	−0.6	6.4
Purchasing power of exports(c)	5.9	5.0	7.3	2.8	1.1	−1.2	8.7	12.6
Budget deficit/GDP	n.a.	−3.1	−3.6	−3.3	−4.0	−4.8	−4.6	−4.0
Growth of broad money aggregates	n.a.	30.9	42.5	36.5	40.1	40.5	47.5	54.1
Inflation rate, CPI	26.4	20.8	24.8	31.4	30.0	30.1	41.4	47.4
III. *External financial policy*								
Import cover (months)(d)	2.9	3.2	2.7	2.2	2.0	2.0	2.4	2.6
Growth of external debt	22.4	17.6	18.6	20.5	18.1	13.3	5.8	5.3
Average interest cost (%)(e)	5.2	5.5	6.7	8.0	9.7	9.8	8.5	8.3
Ratio of debt growth to interest cost (%)	430.8	320.0	277.6	256.3	186.6	135.7	68.2	63.9
Net financial transfer/imports (%)(f)	13.4	13.0	9.9	12.3	13.6	4.1	−1.0	−4.4
Short-term debt/imports (months)	2.4	3.0	2.6	2.8	3.3	4.2	3.8	3.3
Capital flight (US $ billion)(g)	4.9	5.4	0.9	13.2	16.5	21.1	9.6	5.3

Notes:
(a) The incremental capital output ratio (ICOR) equals the ratio of investment/GDP to the real growth of GDP.
(b) Computed as the sum of the investment to GDP ratio and the current account deficit to GDP ratio.
(c) Export earnings deflated by import prices; first observation is the compound average rate of change 1967–1976.
(d) Ratio of foreign exchange, SDRs and gold at SDR 35/oz. to average monthly imports of goods and services.
(e) Total interest payments as a percentage of total external debt.
(f) Ratio of gross loan disbursements, less debt service payments to imports of goods only (fob).
(g) Value of recorded deficit on errors and omissions.
(h) Annual arithmetic average.

Sources: IMF, *World Economic Outlook*, 1983, 1985 and 1987 (Tables 8, 13, 30; 5, 6, 15; and 7, respectively).
IMF, *International Financial Statistics: Supplement on Output Statistics*, 1984, pp. 3 and 55.

First, the growth of domestic savings did not match the growth of gross fixed capital formation. As can be seen in Table 2.3, the average ratio of savings to GDP during the periods 1973–1977 and 1978–1981 remained constant at 21.6 per cent. The rising proportion of investment to GDP and a stagnant ratio of savings to GDP increased the foreign exchange resource gap of the non-oil developing countries. Thus, the current account deficit rose from an annual average of 3.2 per cent of GDP during the years 1973–1977 to an average of almost 4.0 per cent during the years 1978–1981. The ratio of investment to GDP began to decline only after the non-oil developing countries faced a supply constraint on external credit. Pursuit of rapid growth of domestic investment combined with stagnant or low growth of domestic savings requires increasing reliance on external debt accumulation which, if unabated, will necessarily end in a foreign credit constraint to output growth. Policies of domestic financial reform were not adequately pursued in the debtor countries, given the observed stagnation in the growth of domestic savings.

The pursuit of an aggressive investment programme is also ill advised due to the limited absorptive capacity of the developing countries. Owing to the absence of a sufficient supply of complementary inputs to production, an excessively rapid rate of capital formation will result in diminishing marginal returns or in a decline in the marginal efficiency of capital. As shown in Table 2.3, the average incremental capital output ratio rose from an average of 4.6 during the years 1973–1977 to 8.7 during the years 1978–1982. Hence, between these two periods the average marginal efficiency of capital fell by over 47 per cent. Compared to the prior period, this decline meant that approximately twice as much investment was required in the latter period to generate the same GDP growth rate for the non-oil developing countries. Reliance on an 'extensive' pattern of growth, wherein the majority of GDP growth is generated by an increase in the supply of physical inputs (for example, capital formation), is unwarranted. Increases in factor productivity or an 'intensive' growth pattern represent the true basis for sustainable increases in real output and income.

The final problem connected with an excessively rapid investment plan is the rigidity it creates in the economy's trade adjustment capability. Much investment spending in developing countries requires a high proportion of imported capital equipment, intermediate goods, raw materials and foreign expertise. Given the extended gestation period of many investments, this essential or non-compressible component of merchandise and service imports will remain high over the life of the investment. For example, from 1979 to 1983, capital equipment, intermediate goods and oil purchases represented 81.4 per cent of total merchandise imports for seven important Latin American debtors (IADB, 1984). If a country experiences a severely tightened foreign-exchange constraint its policy-makers may be faced with the dilemma of cutting politically sensitive compressible imports, non-compressible imports (thus delaying investment plans) or running arrears on external debt service payments. For example, the same group of Latin debtors in the period 1981–83 were virtually evenly divided as to their import policy response; choosing between cutting compressible or non-compressible imports.

Demand Management and Trade Adjustment Policy
In many developing countries throughout the 1960s and 1970s, public sector enterprises were established, supplying new infrastructure, products and services. This raised the government's share of total output and employment in the economy. Owing to a narrow tax base the growth of government revenue quite often lagged behind the growth of government expenditure, especially during periods of rapid economic growth or trade adjustment. The result was rising public sector deficits. Typically, only a small portion of this resource gap was financed by domestic savings, owing to underdeveloped domestic capital markets. The balance was usually covered by foreign borrowing and rapid growth of the broad money supply (that is, domestic credit and M1).

Table 2.3 on p. 32 shows that the non-oil developing countries responded to the second oil shock and the deceleration in the rate of international lending by running larger fiscal deficits and increasing the growth of the broad money aggregates. Concurrent with a fall in trade-based tax revenue, due to slower import and export growth, many governments faced impediments to the reduction of expenditures, thus precluding tighter fiscal policy. When trimming expenditures, it is usually easier for governments to shelve government-sponsored investment programmes than to cut jobs, salaries and price subsidies. Even if the fiscal deficit is reduced, the ratio of capital to current expenditures usually falls, and this worsens economy-wide resource allocation and lowers the country's ultimate ability to service its foreign debt.

Heavy reliance on the growth of domestic credit to fund public and private enterprises results in excessively rapid growth of the money supply and usually leads to a high inflation rate. This, in turn, erodes the international price competitiveness of the export industry (assuming a fixed nominal exchange rate policy) and also creates artificially high demand for imports. Both of these trends will tend to deplete the country's foreign exchange reserves and increase the necessity to borrow external funds.

The faster growth of the money supply, coupled with currency depreciation, dramatically increased the rate of inflation from an average annual rate of 25.4 per cent during the years 1973–1978 to 34.2 per cent during the years 1979–1984. In the most extreme cases, hyperinflation has resulted which so skews resource allocation that much of the productive economic activity is impaired and the social and political institutions of the country are eroded. In such cases poor economic management can result in a change of political regime which may undermine the willingness as well as the ability to repay foreign debt.

The current account grew more quickly than export revenue for the non-oil developing countries owing both to excessive domestic absorption of resources relative to their domestic supply and to the terms-of-trade decline. As is shown in Table 2.3, this was particularly true after the second oil shock in 1979–80. Averaging 18.4 per cent between 1973 and 1979, the current account deficit as a proportion of total export receipts rose to 22.3 per cent in 1980–1981. Starting in late 1981, the externally imposed decline in credit-based import capacity forced a decline in import volume and the deceleration of GDP growth. These trends combined to improve the expenditure-resource imbalance.

While achieving a healthy average annual growth of 6.0 per cent during 1973–1979, the purchasing power of exports or the income terms of trade increased at an average annual rate of only 0.9 per cent in 1980–1982. The strong export performance of the non-oil developing countries after the first oil shock resulted in increased export-based import capacity. The trend of gross export receipts after the second oil shock, however, meant that import volume could be significantly raised only by accelerating external borrowing.

The expenditure switching policies of the non-oil developing countries were inadequate to neutralize the sharp decline in their terms of trade after the second oil shock. After the first oil shock, the growth rates of export volume and import volume were closely matched. After the second oil shock, however, the average annual growth of export volume advanced only 7.1 per cent; a deceleration of over 50 per cent compared to the years 1973–77. Thus, as is shown in Table 2.3, although the growth of export volume exceeded the growth of import demand by an average 1.5 per cent per annum from 1979 to 1981, it was insufficient to avoid a widening of the current account deficit. Due to the severity of the terms-of-trade decline and due to the persistence of over-valued exchange rates, the non-oil developing countries could increase their import volume only through the growth of external credit after 1979.

Since the commodity composition of merchandise imports for

certain indebted developing countries was not carefully controlled, external borrowings were not always used to purchase goods and services which enhanced the productive capacity of the debtor. For example, during the years 1979–1981 the growth of imported consumer goods for key Latin American debtors (for example, Argentina, Brazil, Chile, Colombia, Mexico, Peru and Venezuela) rose an average 77.7 per cent. During the same period, non-compressible imports such as capital goods, intermediate goods and oil purchases lagged behind this rate, increasing 35.2 per cent, 57.9 per cent, and 58.5 per cent, respectively (IADB, 1984). Moreover, once stabilization policies were implemented during the period 1981–1983, the rate of decline in import expenditures on consumer goods for several of these countries was less than that for expenditures on imported capital equipment.

External Financial Policy
The excessive resource gap (that is, the current account deficit plus amortization payments) of the non-oil developing countries during the 1970s resulted in the rapid accumulation of external debt. Domar (1950) found that a debtor country's external liabilities will reach a finite limit and the country eventually will become a net creditor if the growth of external debt remains below the average interest rate on external borrowing. According to this stability requirement, the borrowing record of the non-oil developing countries never was stable. As can be seen in Table 2.3 on p. 32 the growth of external debt exceeded the average cost of the debt in every year from 1973 to 1982. Only when the growth of external debt was constrained by the international creditors did the ratio fall to a level which met this necessary condition for long-term financial stability. Thus, the non-oil developing countries relied too heavily on the accumulation of foreign liabilities rather than trade adjustment as a policy response to the changing international environment of the 1970s.

Not only did the growth of total external debt expand more quickly than was prudent but an excessive amount of short-term maturities also were accumulated, especially after the second oil shock. Although the average proportion of short-term debt increased from 14.1 per cent of total debt in 1973 to 16.3 per cent in 1979, its magnitude remained broadly consistent with the level of import expenditures during this period. During 1973 to 1979 the average value of short-term debt owed by the non-oil developing countries was equivalent to 2.5 months of merchandise imports. On the assumption that short-term debt primarily finances international trade flows, the outstanding level of these liabilities should not exceed the equivalent of three months of imports which is consistent with a portfolio of trade credits with an average ninety-day tenor.

After the second oil price shock the non-oil developing countries relied too heavily on new short-term liabilities, an increasing proportion of which rolled over medium and long-term amortization payments. During the period from the end of 1979 to the end of 1982, the ratio of short-term debt to total debt jumped from 16.3 per cent to 20.1 per cent. Thus, during these three years the average annual rate of short-term debt accumulation exceeded that of longer term debt by nearly 70 per cent. As can be seen in Table 2.3 on p. 32 the average value of outstanding short-term debt rose to an equivalent of 3.5 months of merchandise import expenditures during 1980–83, reaching a peak of 4.2 months in 1982. Such levels of short-term debt are well beyond the threshold for a prudent sovereign external balance sheet.

While the proportion of short-term liabilities to import expenditures was increasing, the ratio of foreign exchange reserves to imports was falling. Import cover is defined as the number of average months of import expenditure on goods and services which the year-end stock of foreign exchange reserves will finance. Normally, international creditors expect a prudent borrower to maintain an import cover of three months. Although the non-oil developing countries possessed an average import cover of three months during the period of 1973–1978, this level fell to an average of only 2.2 months from 1979 to 1984, reaching its nadir of only two months in 1981 and 1982. Hence, an increase in short-term liabilities and a fall in short-term assets relative to current import expenditures resulted in a marked deterioration of the external balance sheets of the non-oil developing countries after the second oil shock.

Another error of the non-oil developing countries was to pursue policies which increased the likelihood of capital flight. Within an environment of rapid price inflation, a policy of low nominal interest rates and a fixed exchange rate will result in negative real interest rates and an overvalued currency. This financial repression discourages the mobilization of domestic savings and creates expectations for a currency devaluation which will result in capital flight.

Assuming that the recorded errors and omissions' deficit in the balance of payments for the non-oil developing countries is a measure of these unrecorded capital outflows, the amount of capital flight was excessive.[3] From 1973 to 1984, this cumulative deficit on the capital account of non-oil developing countries totalled US $96.5 billion, or 13.2 per cent of the total disbursed external debt as of year-end 1984. Allowing external debt accumulation to finance capital flight is wholly inappropriate, expecially since capital flight can be minimized by an appropriate set of domestic financial policies.

As is shown in Table 2.3 on p. 32 the pace of capital flight from the non-oil developing countries quickened after the second oil shock, owing to their increasingly overvalued currencies. The average annual outflow of US $14.9 billion during 1980 and 1981 equalled approximately 28 per cent of the net financial transfer in each of these years. With the outflow increasing to US $21.1 billion in 1982, it represented a full 137.9 per cent of the net financial transfer from external creditors. Thus, in that year the net resource flow to the non-oil developing countries wholly financed capital flight. If the estimated US $96.5 billion of capital flight was to be repatriated to the developing countries it could finance almost three years of current account deficits, given the present average shortfall.

2.4   Debt Rescheduling as a Debtor Country Policy Response

Given the already high levels of external debt by early 1981, the combination of cumulative economic policy errors and numerous external shocks to the non-oil developing countries resulted in borrowing requirements which were too large to be sustained. During 1981, almost two years after the second oil shock, the current account deficit of the non-oil developing countries was still increasing and the net financial transfer reached a peak of US $57 billion. Despite an attempt by the external creditors to recycle OPEC money at ever increasing levels, these unprecedented financial flows were insufficient to meet the borrowing requirements of the non-oil developing countries.

Despite decelerating GDP growth rates and falling import volume in developing countries, the expenditure-resource imbalance remained unstable due to decelerating export growth, rapidly deteriorating terms of trade and accelerating capital flight. Although adjustment had begun, the degree of stabilization required meant that the developing country policy-makers were faced with the prospect of drastically reducing non-compressible imports and thus investment programmes, or delaying debt service payments, or both. A combination of the two occurred, and accordingly in 1980 and 1981 the value of arrears rose by 100 per cent and 150 per cent, respectively. This signalled to the creditors that the debt recycling process was unsustainable. Thus, in 1982 the growth of new lending decelerated sharply and further trade adjustment for the non-oil developing countries was externally induced by the restriction of credit-supply.

Once the limits to borrowing were reached, the incidence of arrears among indebted countries accelerated. For example in 1982, when the net financial transfer fell by 73 per cent, arrears increased over threefold. With an approximate two-year lag, the number of debt rescheduling agreements also increased substantially. As can be seen in Table 2.4, the value of debt relief, which includes the amount of rescheduled arrears, future debt service payments and new money facilities, rose exponentially from US $2.6 billion in 1981 to US $199.2 billion in 1984. Many of these reschedulings represent repeat occurrences by the same country, since the necessity of extended relief meant that the one- to two-year rescheduling agreements were inadequate.

Since sufficient leverage existed but was not exercised, the non-oil developing countries committed another external financial policy error by not obtaining a debt rescheduling package from the external creditors which was sufficiently concessional.

Given that many of the impaired debtor countries were suffering not only from illiquidity but also from insolvency, the need for a long-term agreement was apparent. This meant that the rescheduling agreement should have incorporated more than just accumulated arrears and the next twelve months of scheduled payments. The new negotiated agreement should have encompassed the amortization payments due over the next five years or longer and should have spread these payments over a sufficiently long period. The inability to obtain adequate debt relief from both the official and private creditors resulted in autocorrelated rescheduling agreements. The insufficient terms of debt rescheduling necessitated repeated rescheduling agreements, thus increasing administrative costs and creating unrealistic expectations of a short-term solution to what is a long-term problem.

Although the non-oil developing countries have reduced their borrowing requirements every year after 1981, their access to external credit has also diminished sharply over the same period. While the growth of bank lending (Bank for International Settlements reporting banks) grew an average of 24.9 per cent per annum from 1973 to 1981, it advanced an average of only 5.6 per cent from 1982 to 1984 (IMF, 1985b). During this latter period its growth rate continued to decelerate, reaching a new low of only 2 per cent in 1984. It is likely that little of this growth is voluntary, since debt rescheduling agreements typically require new money facilities. This absence of voluntary lending by the private international commercial banks signals a disruption in the intermediation process, particularly given the leading role they played from 1973 to 1981.

Key multilateral agencies, such as the IMF, World Bank and

Table 2.4 Incidence and Magnitude of Debt Servicing Difficulties, 1975–1984 (as indicated)

	1975	1976	1977	1978	1979	1980	1981	1982	1983	1984
I. *Incidence of debt rescheduling*										
Total agreements (a)	2	2	3	6	7	8	13	15	38	44
Multilateral reschedulings (b)	2	2	3	3	4	3	7	6	16	13
Private reschedulings (c)	0	0	3	3	3	5	6	9	22	31
Total debtor countries involved	2	2	2	4	5	8	12	12	26	28
II. *Magnitude of debt rescheduling*										
Arrears (US$ billion)	0.0	0.0	1.6	0.5	0.4	0.8	2.0	6.6	2.3	0.9
Value of debt relief (US$ million)(d)	387	439	249	2,232	6,241	4,665	2,647	10,162	75,744	199,156
Debt relief/total debt (%)	0.2	0.2	0.1	0.7	1.5	1.0	0.5	1.6	10.9	27.3

Notes:

(a) A debtor country with two agreements in the same year is classified as two separate debt reschedulings.

(b) Represents primarily Paris Club reschedulings amongst other official creditor groups.

(c) Represents private commercial bank reschedulings only.

(d) Defined as the sum of rescheduled arrears and future principal and interest payments and new loan disbursements.

Sources: IMF, Recent Developments in External Debt Restructuring, 1985, Tables 3, 4 and 17.

regional development banks, have increased the pace of their lending, especially since 1981. In addition, the Bank for International Settlements and certain bilateral agencies have directly supplied short-term bridge financing at crucial times to the illiquid developing countries. Although this lending has been an important factor in avoiding the spectre of default or repudiation, it is unlikely that such official agencies can supply adequate amounts of financing to the non-oil developing countries over a long-term period. As a result, the risks of international lending have increased significantly and the quality of the current outstanding claims of international lenders on some developing countries is questionable.

Since the risks of international lending have increased, it is important to improve the methods for assessing sovereign credit risk (that is, country risk analysis). Only after this has been accomplished and a positive net financial transfer to the developing countries renewed will a viable long-term solution to the current international debt crisis be found and the prospects be improved for a return to positive secular growth and development in the developing debtor countries.

End-Chapter Notes

1   The inability of high real interest rates to bring down the inflation rate more quickly may have been due, in part, to price rigidities in the factor markets (for example, downward stickiness of wages). Thus, this factor-market rigidity contributed to the persistence of high real interest rates.

2   The six-month US $ inter-bank deposit rate in London (LIBOR) was deflated by the growth of export unit values for non-oil developing countries.

3   Such a measure is likely to understate the actual amount of capital flight.

PART II

Sovereign Creditworthiness and Debt Early-Warning Systems

3.
External Debt Accumulation and Rescheduling Risk

3.1 Introduction

The necessity for developing countries to supplement domestic resources with foreign savings to hasten the process of growth and development creates continuous demand for international credit. International banks constantly have to create new financial claims to ensure long-term profitability. Hence, the vast financial requirements of the developing world, coupled with the banks' need for constant asset growth, should create a symbiotic relationship.

With any investment opportunity, however, there exists a certain degree of risk for both the debtor and the creditor. In this case, the risk to the developing countries is that their access to new international credit will be curtailed before the development cycle is complete, thus necessitating severe retrenchment, recession and possible political unrest. The attendant risk to the international private creditors is that poor economic and financial policies or a series of global shocks will disrupt financial intermediation, resulting in debt service payment arrears, non-performing assets and stagnation of earnings. The worst case scenario is when the borrower defaults or repudiates its obligation to repay its foreign debt. This action severely weakens bank earnings, erodes bank capital, and possibly results in increased government regulation of the industry or even insolvency and nationalization of certain banks.

It is in the interest of both the developing countries and the international banking community to maintain a sustainable process of debt accumulation, including a smooth flow of new lending and timely repayment of debt service obligations. For this to occur, the developing countries must pursue policies which establish the economic foundations for sustainable borrowing so that their debt will be repaid according to its contracted terms. The banks, in order to assess sovereign credit risk and manage their international loan portfolio, also need a clear understanding of the economic foundations of sovereign debt service capacity. This requires a robust credit scoring system based on economic theory which can produce an objective relative risk rating of sovereign debtors.

3.2   The Scope of Sovereign Credit Risk Analysis

The sustained growth of international trade, economic integration, and thus the diffusion of economic development to the developing countries, all depend on the concomitant growth and increased sophistication of global financial intermediation. The smooth and continuous flow of financial capital, ranging from short-term trade finance to long-term national development bonds, is required to facilitate this increased interdependence among the economies of sovereign nations. Ad hoc management of international financial exposure by private commercial banks, based more on ambitious growth goals than on prudent portfolio decisions, proved to be increasingly inadequate throughout the 1970s as the depth and breadth of international sovereign lending dramatically increased due, in part, to the international transmission of oil price shocks.[1]

Cognizant of these shortcomings, international financial institutions began to improve portfolio management techniques during the latter half of the 1970s by refining and expanding the use of country risk analysis. This shift required analysts to forecast more accurately a country's likelihood of debt rescheduling. Within this milieu, traditional approaches of creditworthiness assessment involving heuristic or unstructured analysis were re-examined and in many cases supplemented with more systematic and quantitative methods.[2]

Part III of this book develops an operational theory of sovereign debt rescheduling risk assessment. It facilitates a more systematic approach to country risk analysis, thereby achieving active portfolio management and minimizing the risk of impaired assets due to rescheduling or default. Improving the efficiency of portfolio management and international capital allocation will help renew voluntary lending and overcome the current impasse in global financial intermediation which has been especially acute since August 1982.

Sovereign credit risk or country risk analysis is concerned with political and economic factors which can interrupt the sustainable flow of international lending between sovereign nations and the timely repayment of principal and interest according to the terms of the original loan agreement. Repayment of loan obligations requires both the ability and the willingness of the debtor country to maintain its international credit standing. While the model presented in this book addresses both the willingness and the ability of the debtor to repay its external liabilities, it does not explicitly incorporate any political factors which may motivate the debtor's behaviour.[3]

The model presented in Chapter 5 predicts the likelihood of debt rescheduling based on key economic variables, including both exogenous factors and predetermined debtor country policy variables. The observed rescheduling behaviour of debtor countries is assumed to be an explicit policy decision. Each debtor country formulates a complex decision-making strategy based on its long-term development goals, medium-term adjustment requirements, short-term external financial preferences and the global economic environment. Arriving at this strategy requires decisions concerning development goals, exchange rate regime, the mix of demand management policy in an open economy, balance of payments financing methods and, ultimately, the choice of rescheduling mode (that is, whether to run arrears and request a debt rescheduling or continue to service the external debt according to its contractual terms). Thus, the likelihood of a debt rescheduling or the developing country's demand for rescheduling is a function both of its assessment of its own incremental progress toward long-term development goals and of changes in its preference for intertemporal resource allocation, given the constantly changing international economy and the shocks which this environment transmits.

Most of the quantitative studies have focused primarily on the immediate foreign-exchange cash-flow determinants of rescheduling risk. Only the surface phenomena are measured by looking at indicators such as exports, import cover, debt levels, debt service payments and the net financial transfer. The underlying factors which determine the need to borrow and the propensity to lend are not emphasized or altogether ignored. From the debtor country's perspective, however, all the aforementioned facets of the growth-cum-indebtedness process are interrelated with the decision to begin and to continue borrowing abroad. For example, were a debtor country to decide to pursue a more autarchic development strategy, the debtor's perceived cost of an external credit embargo and thus a credit-imposed import reduction would clearly diminish. Since changes in development goals, among other factors, can affect debtor behaviour by altering the perceived cost of rescheduling or default, an attempt must be made to incorporate these underlying factors into the model to obtain a comprehensive approach to country risk analysis.

Smooth international financial intermediation also requires the elastic supply of credit. Clearly, the inelastic supply of new international credit has exacerbated the debt crisis since 1982. Hence, the econometric specification must include a variable which measures the creditor's willingness to lend.

3.3 The Objectives of Modelling Sovereign Credit Risk

Successful portfolio diversification to minimize risk requires an efficient credit-scoring methodology. This requirement led to a spate of analytical techniques during the 1970s to assess sovereign creditworthiness. These range from those which are strictly qualitative and subjective to those which are entirely quantitative.

The strength of both the unstructured and the structured qualitative methods is that they provide an in-depth analysis of political and economic performance for a particular country. Although most widely used, the non-quantitative approachs do not easily facilitate an objective cross-country comparison of creditworthiness. So although a fairly accurate picture of an individual country can be obtained from this approach, assessing its position relative to other countries at any point in time is somewhat problematical. Nor do these two methods take an adequately prospective approach to debt service capacity. Since there is no systematic methodology for combining or weighing the relevant macroeconomic trends of the economy, it is sometimes difficult to assess what the combination of projected cash-flow indicators means for the country's rescheduling probability.

The checklist approach explicitly defines a crucial group of factors which affect the country's future debt service capacity. This systematic approach represents an improvement over the qualitative approach by allowing a definitive comparison of trends across countries. In addition, this methodology can also incorporate non-economic factors. Despite these improvements, the checklist approach retains one shortcoming of the qualitative approach. The process of selecting the creditworthiness indicators and their respective weights, which is required to compute the composite rating, remains subjective. Since the weighting of the respective variables in the checklist may not be correct, the projected composite creditworthiness is unreliable.

By contrast, the fully quantitative or econometric approach to creditworthiness improves upon the prior methods by achieving an objective cross-country comparison and by being prospective. The selection and weighting of the explanatory variables is arrived at by proven statistical methods.

Data limitations and the conceptual limitations of incorporating political factors remain inherent weaknesses of the quantitative approach. Moreover, many of these studies published over the past decade have suffered from one of several other avoidable shortcomings. These problems include: the absence of an adequate theoretical foundation; a poor definition of the dependent variable; a restrictively small data base which has an inadequate number of dependent variable data points; and, occasionally, inappropriate statistical methodology. This book attempts to address some of these shortcomings by developing a probabilistic choice model of international debt rescheduling based on a formal utility framework. The model specification is determined by economic theory while the hypotheses are tested using multivariate statistics and various econometric methods on panel data (that is, time series and cross section). The data base covers most of the significant developing country debtors from 1971 to 1984.

The ability of a sovereign debt early warning model to accurately forecast outside the original sample requires that it incorporate the crucial causal relationships. It must establish the behavioural connection between the debtor's current rescheduling decision (that is, run arrears or repay scheduled debt service) and both the current characteristics of the external financial environment, the country's performance and its economic policy stance. The behavioural aspect of the model incorporates the debtor's choice (and its reformulation over time) between the alternative rescheduling modes, each of which, in turn, are subject to complementary decisions concerning economic policy issues. In subsequent time periods, the respective cost of the rescheduling modes can change, the attribute values of the complementary decisions can be altered, or other relevant exogenous global factors may change. To highlight these changing environmental or contingent elements, each country-year is treated as an individual observation in the model. The use of panel data increases the sample size, country composition and degrees of freedom, all of which will impart more information concerning the underlying population, thus facilitating more accurate calibration of the model.

In this book, the rescheduling observation is defined to include any known case in which contractual cross-border debt service payments to bilateral, multilateral, or private lending institutions either fall into arrears, are repudiated, rescheduled, or refinanced.[4] Refinancings which were deemed 'voluntary' were not included since they represent a normal facet of external financial policy.[5] This formulation contains 114 rescheduling observations covering forty countries over the period between 1971 to 1984.[6]

The predicted values of the model's dependent variable are interpreted as the debtor country's probability of debt repayment difficulties, as just defined. This composite indicator of rescheduling risk can be used to construct an objective uni-dimensional ranking of two or more debtor countries according to their economic creditworthiness. In this manner, a country's debt service capacity relative to another country (*discrete cross-sectional creditworthiness*) can be ascertained for any single point in time. Looking at the trend in the relative ranking of an individual country over time highlights the change in its temporal debt service capacity relative to other countries (*dynamic cross-sectional creditworthiness*).

This model can also be used to assess a debtor country's absolute debt service capacity. The point estimate of rescheduling probability can stand alone as the predicted likelihood of the country experiencing debt service difficulties (*discrete absolute creditworthiness*). The change in the country's rescheduling probability over time measures its current debt service capacity relative to its own past or future performance (*dynamic absolute creditworthiness*).

The retrospective classification efficiency of the model can be assessed by comparing estimated with actual rescheduling experience. An estimated rescheduling probability which exceeds a chosen cut-off value is classified as a rescheduling observation. In this manner, all country-years can be divided into rescheduling and non-rescheduling observations. The model's efficiency is measured in terms of Type I (false non-rescheduling prediction) and Type II (false rescheduling prediction) error rates. An identical test can be performed on either hold-out data or stochastic data to assess the predictive classification efficiency of the model.

Depending upon the needs of the portfolio manager, the model can be applied to a number of projects ranging from portfolio management, loan pricing and discounting non-performing assets for sale or swap in a secondary market. Part II of this book reviews the issues related to building a quantitative sovereign credit-scoring model and creating a debt early-warning system. The model specification is based on a Lancaster-type utility framework and tested with data from the 1970s and 1980s. Chapter 7 in Part III will discuss current issues to debt early warning systems and their financial applications.

The extent of the current impasse in international financial intermediation is reflected by the growing number of reschedulings involving larger amounts of debt. While a lasting solution to this crisis involves concerted action by many key participants, the ability and willingness of commercial banks to renew voluntary international lending remains a crucial element.[7] For this to occur these institutions must have a better system to monitor and assess sovereign credit risk in order to minimize the loss from bad assets.

While certain risk factors that contributed to the current debt crisis were systematic or global in nature, others were clearly country specific or non-systematic.[8] Goodman (1981) found that country-specific risk factors were more important than global or common risk factors during the 1970s. Casual examination of relative country performance of debt servicing supports her finding.

While certain global or systematic factors worsened significantly from 1979 to 1983, heavily indebted developing countries were not universally affected. Unlike other large debtors, the Republic of Korea has not fallen into arrears as yet. Moreover, within this difficult environment other debtors with past rescheduling problems (for example, Turkey) have been able to improve their economic performance and international credit standing since 1980. Thus, on the assumption that non-systematic or country-specific factors largely determine any particular sovereign rescheduling risk, portfolio diversification remains a useful financial tool. A quantitative debt early warning system is a necessary component of efficient portfolio management.

End-Chapter Notes

1 Other important factors underlying the rapid growth of international lending during the 1970s include: (1) an excess supply of loanable funds in the domestic financial markets of OECD countries and in the Eurocurrency market due to weak demand for credit from traditional sources; (2) a short-fall of the developing countries' export revenue owing to declining terms-of-trade and weak export demand; and (3) the inability and unwillingness of certain developing countries to lower development targets, reduce domestic demand, import expenditures and capital flight.

2 In 1976, the Export-Import Bank compiled data on the types of country evaluation systems in use by US banks. These evaluation systems were divided into four categories based on their methodology, namely, fully qualitative, structured qualitative, checklist and fully quantitative. While most of the banks in the survey used the structured qualitative approach, some banks used a combination of methods to improve the assessment. Other banks indicated they were reviewing current methodologies and organizational structures. A small proportion of the respondents used no system whatsoever. Friedman, 1983 suggests the use of an integrated and comprehensive system which includes both structured qualitative and quantitative (i.e. econometric) methods. See Haendel, 1979 and Rogers, 1983 for methodologies focusing specifically on the management of political-related risk.

3 Explicit political factors which affect a country's willingness or ability to repay foreign debt are omitted from this book. Certain economic factors are included, however, which indirectly measure the government's political legitimacy and thus the regime's stability. For example, the relative purchasing power parity index which incorporates politically sensitive decisions such as a currency devaluation is included in the quantitative model presented in Chapter 5. A comprehensive assessment of a country's rescheduling probability requires a full political analysis to complement the economic and financial aspects. Since many relevant political variables cannot be easily quantified or forecast, they

cannot be dealt with easily in an econometric model. Nonetheless, the creation of dummy variables based on subjective assessments of political trends can be used. In addition, weighted probability trees and other quasi-quantitative methods are available. These conceptual and data limitations suggest that a comprehensive approach to country risk analysis requires both a quantitative and a structured qualitative assessment to adequately address all of the relevant risks.

4   These various situations are defined as follows: (1) *arrears* – overdue cross-border interest or amortization payments; (2) *repudiation* – abrogation of legal responsibility for repayment of external debt; (3) *rescheduling* – renegotiation of the original loan contract so that the amortization structure and/or the grace period are lengthened to facilitate repayment, while the loan's price (that is, interest rate, supplementary fees, etc.) may or may not be raised despite the increased risk; (4) *distressed refinancing* – a disbursement of a new loan which is used to repay debt service obligations on a prior loan without which arrears would have arisen.

5   'Voluntary' refinancings result from a preference to lower the average cost of outstanding debt by prematurely retiring old debt with new cheaper borrowing. 'Involuntary' refinancings by contrast occur during a liquidity squeeze and are used to repay debt service obligations on old debt without which arrears would have occurred. In practice, distinguishing between these two cases can be difficult. In this book these two types of refinancing were distinguished according to the definition presented by Porzecanski, 1980.

6   These rescheduling observations were constructed from a variety of sources which include Bitterman, 1973; Hardy, 1982; IMF, 1981a; IMF, 1983a; IMF, 1985b; Mendelson, 1983; OECD, 1979b; OECD, 1982; Wall Street Journal, various issues.

7   Other important agents also have critical roles which must be met to achieve a genuine solution to the debt crisis. These include: (1) continued adjustment programmes in the developing countries; (2) sustained recovery and lower protectionism in the developed countries; (3) increased capitalization of and lending by the IMF, the IBRD and other multilateral agencies; and (4) continued extension of bridge financing by the Bank for International Settlements, reserve-currency central banks, or finance ministries to illiquid countries which have not finalized an adequate debt rescheduling agreement.

8   Systematic risk factors are those which affect the international markets as a whole and thus are common to all debtor countries. Non-systematic risk factors are those which exclusively affect an individual country's debt service capacity. While the former type of risk is non-diversifiable, there are portfolio management techniques which can entirely eliminate non-systematic risk from a loan portfolio.

4.
Credit-Scoring Techniques and Country Risk Analysis

4.1 Introduction

This chapter presents a selective critical review of the statistically-based debt early warning models developed during the 1970s and early 1980s. The chapter is issue-oriented to highlight the strengths and weaknesses of key aspects of quantitative credit-scoring techniques for country risk analysis. The credit-scoring model's theoretical structure, its data requirements, definition of the rescheduling variable and the appropriate statistical technique are all addressed.

4.2 A Survey of Quantitative Sovereign Credit-Scoring Models

The Export-Import Bank conducted a survey in 1977 of thirty-seven US banks in an attempt to establish the nature and scope of the industry's sovereign credit risk evaluation process. The group polled, which included the twelve largest banks, accounted for almost 30 per cent of the US banking industry's total assets and over half of its international loans. The results revealed that the analytical approaches to sovereign risk evaluation varied widely. Nonetheless, four broad types of credit-scoring systems are distinguished. These approaches are: (1) fully qualitative; (2) structured qualitative; (3) checklist, and (4) other quantitative.

The *fully qualitative system* did not use any type of fixed format whatsoever. The analytical content of each report varied widely from country to country. While allowing for an in-depth analysis of an individual country's creditworthiness, this approach is seriously weakened by its ad hoc nature. Without a consistent framework of analysis for every country, the ability to make required cross-country comparisons is hindered. The viewpoint of these evaluations also tended to be too retrospective rather than prospective which limits the early warning aspect of the analysis. Because of these limitations, only 11 per cent of the polled banks, representing a mere 4 per cent of the total assets of the sample, exclusively utilized this approach.[1]

The *structured qualitative approach* produced a report with a standardized format and well-defined scope. Economic data was used to obtain a detailed individual country assessment. While comparisons across countries are possible because of the standardized format, the strength of this approach is clearly the analysis of an individual country's prospects over time. Since the translation of the individual country assessment into a global sovereign credit ranking remains wholly subjective, portfolio decisions will not be reliable. A full 62 per cent of the sample, representing 74 per cent of the banks' assets, used such an approach.

The third credit-scoring method encompassed the *weighted or unweighted checklist*. This approach incorporates a group of economic, financial, social and political indicators which are compiled for all surveyed countries. Each variable is subjectively weighted according to the analyst's preferred emphasis on relevant factors. The variables are quantitative or quantifiable and thus can be aggregated into a composite statistic or summary rating for each country. While highlighting the comparative aspects of credit scoring, this approach is impaired by the subjective method of variable selection and weighting for the composite statistic. None of the surveyed banks used this technique as their sole method of analysis, although 11 per cent of the banks, accounting for 4 per cent of the sample's total assets, used the checklist in conjunction with the structured qualitative approach.

The final method of analysis involved *other quantitative techniques*. Econometric or other statistical methodologies were employed to choose and weight the relevant explanatory variables objectively. This technique potentially offers the most objective, systematic and comparative approach to assess a country's creditworthiness. Despite its advantages, only 2 per cent of the banks polled, representing 11 per cent of total bank assets, used this method, and even these banks used it only in conjunction with the checklist system. The fact that so few commercial banks, albeit with a larger share of assets, used this technique in the mid 1970s is a reflection of the high cost of mobilizing resources for this system, particularly given the rudimentary state of the art at that time.

During the latter 1970s, an increasing number of quantitative models were constructed which classified sovereign debtors according to their historical or prospective creditworthiness. By applying various statistical methods to the analysis of sovereign debt-service capacity, these studies represented a fundamental methodological improvement over earlier heuristic works.[2] Despite this improvement, numerous deficiencies of the quantitative approach were apparent, such as the neglect of its underlying theoretical structure, a limited data base, an inadequate rescheduling definition, and in some cases inappropriate statistical methodology. Nonetheless, as the foundations of sovereign debt service capacity have become better understood, as data availability has improved and as quantitative techniques have become refined, these limitations have diminished. The inherent methodological superiority of this approach bodes well for the broader application of these quantitative methods in the financial industry.

The importance of a sovereign credit scoring system is reflected not only in its widespread use by 86 per cent of polled banks but also by its numerous applications. Over 70 per cent of the sample banks used some form of country risk analysis to set maximum loan exposure ceilings and sometimes sub-limits for individual countries in their international loan portfolio. Although many banks were dissatisfied with their current country evaluation procedures, its fundamental role in credit scoring, exposure management, loan pricing and industry regulation ensures its continued, indeed increasing, importance for international creditors.

Theoretical Structure
The most serious inadequacy of the quantitative studies is the absence of an explicit *a priori* theoretical structure determining the model specification. Without such a foundation, the initial selection of independent variables proceeds on an ad hoc basis. Data analysis motivated by simple empirical measurement and unguided by theory will result in specification bias. Although this trial-and-error approach can result in relatively efficient historical classification error rates (see Table 4.1), such results are not necessarily indicative of the model's prognosticative efficacy.

Only two of the studies listed in Table 4.1 attempt to identify statistically a particular type of debt servicing problem. Dhonte (1974) looks at short-term liquidity factors and Sargen (1977) investigates medium-term adjustment aspects of creditworthiness. Using principal component analysis, Dhonte analyzes the roll-over process 'of securing a net transfer by obtaining new loans in amounts in excess of debt servicing obligations'. Sargen, in contrast, differentiates between a debt service and a monetary approach to debt rescheduling by using multivariate discriminant analysis.

Among ten initially selected indicators, Dhonte found six which possess reasonable explanatory power. The first four ratios (debt disbursements to imports, net transfer to imports, debt outstanding to exports and debt outstanding to GNP) were strongly and positively correlated with the first principal component which accounted for 38 per cent of the sample's variance (this statistical

Table 4.1 Sample Characteristics of Debt Early-Warning Systems

Model	Number of countries in sample	Number of reschedulings (number of countries)	Time period	Number of sample points	Initial number of explanatory variables (final)	Type I and Type II error rates	
Frank & Cline (1971)	26	13(8)	1960–1968	145	8(3)	23%	11%
Dhonte (1974)	81	12(11)	1959–1971	81	10(6)	33%	13%
Grinols (1976)	n.a.	n.a.	1961–1974	n.a.	20(5)	12%	6%
Feder & Just (1976)	41	21(11)	1965–1972	238	9(6)	5%	3%
Sargen (1977)	67	24(14)	1969–1975	466	6(2)	33%	8%
Mayo & Barret (1977)	48	28(11)	1960–1975	571	50(6)	25%	13%
Smith (1977)[a]	—	—	—	—	—	30%	17%
						10%	13%
Saini & Bates (1978)	25	22(12)	1960–1977	24–173	11(4)	5.5%[b]	
Fisk & Rimlinger (1979)	n.a.	n.a.	n.a.	n.a.	n.a.	28%[b]	
Feder, Just & Ross (1981)	56	40(11)	1965–1976	580	6(6)	8%	9%
Cline (1984)	60	22(16)	1968–1982	670	10(10)	12%	14%

Notes:

(a) Unlisted columns are identical to the Frank & Cline and Feder & Just models since this study reconfirmed their work; The classification efficiency rates are tested on 'hold-out' data covering 1969–1972, and 1976 for the Frank & Cline paper and 1970 and 1976 for the Feder & Just study.

(b) Equally weighted average composite error rates.

technique will be presented in detail later in this section). Dhonte postulated that this group of variables measures a country's 'debt involvement'. Involvement in debt comprises both the country's stock magnitude of debt and its dependence on capital inflows. The two additional significant ratios (debt service to debt outstanding and debt service to debt disbursements) were positively correlated with the second principal component which accounted for another 18 per cent of the sample's variance. This second group of variables measured the 'borrowing conditions' or the terms of the accumulated liabilities and the country's ability to roll-over or refinance these debt service requirements.

Using this conceptualization of the two significant principal components, Dhonte formulates the following hypothesis: there is a trade-off between involvement in debt and borrowing conditions. Difficulties can be expected when a heavy involvement in debt is accompanied by unfavourable borrowing conditions. When tested against the sample data, this hypothesis produced less than average classification error rates. The Type I error rate (false non-rescheduling prediction) was 33 per cent; the Type II error rate (false rescheduling prediction) was 13 per cent.

Unfortunately, Dhonte's methodology is better suited to explain how all the explanatory variables are mutually related rather than to predict whether a country is likely to reschedule. The trial-and-error method of selection for the explanatory variables also limits the usefulness of this approach. An objective specification of a structural econometric model is precluded which, in turn, makes the various principal components virtually impossible to interpret. This arbitrary element of variable selection leads to specification bias and unstable classification and prediction error rates.

Sargen (1977) advances the country-risk literature by segmenting past reschedulings into two conceptual categories (for example, a debt-service and a monetary approach) and statistically testing this hypothesis. The debt-service approach is derived from Avramovic, et al. (1964). This theory focuses on a country's heavy reliance on primary product exports, volatility of foreign exchange earnings, and its inability to reduce non-compressible imports or draw too heavily on a limited supply of international reserves. This shortfall of foreign exchange earnings results in rapid debt accumulation and eventual repayment difficulties. In contrast to this largely exogenous causality, the monetary approach focuses more on the debtor country's economic policy stance or other endogenous factors. It examines domestic price performance, exchange-rate policies, and their impact upon export competitiveness, capital movements, debt accumulation and debt service capacity.

Sargen's results suggest that the inflation rate and the adjusted debt-service ratio (scheduled not actual payments) are the most important rescheduling indicators. According to his schema, the inflation rate acts as an indicator for 'liquidity' reschedulings or those associated with monetary disequilibria. The adjusted debt service ratio classifies 'debt-service' reschedulings.[3] In comparison with the Dhonte study, the 41 per cent overall error rate of Sargen's model showed an improvement. A Type I error rate of 33 per cent was among the highest, while his Type II error rate of 8 per cent was relatively low. The fundamental contribution of Sargen's study is its attempt to differentiate and empirically substantiate the debt-service and monetary approaches to the rescheduling problems of debtor countries.

The other statistical studies in Table 4.1 on p. 56 simply identify a stable empirical relationship between a country's rescheduling probability and myriad economic indicators over a relatively small pooled sample. Therefore, these are not behavioural models since they are not specified according to an *a priori* economic theoretical structure which systematically identifies the rescheduling decision-making process. The pioneering statistical work by Frank and Cline (1971) acknowledged that, 'the purpose of this paper is [to] . . . try to determine the predictive performance of some widely used debt-service indicators. Behind the composite index . . . is an economic story which takes place in terms of stochastic money flows and accounting balances and surpluses'. Without the use of economic theory to provide *a priori* restrictions on structural parameters, however, the estimated empirical relationship is unlikely to be robust. The model's predictive ability will be diminished not only by the usual standard error but also by specification bias and shifts in the structural parameters.

Data and the Sampling Procedure

A second set of difficulties which these studies must overcome encompasses data limitations. Such limitations include: the quality and availability of data for the construction of rescheduling indicators, the arbitrary reduction of the sample space both across countries and time and the lack of consistency and comparability of indicators across countries.

While the economic data of developing countries has improved since 1981, both in terms of quality and breadth of coverage, numerous deficiencies remain. Typically, the availability of macro-economic data on debtor countries is delayed one full year or more. Frequently, gaps can also exist in the time series of a particular country. Errors in measurement are quite common in developing countries' national accounts data, although external accounts data, perhaps, are more accurate. Moreover, it is common for countries to revise both sets of data several years after they were originally published. Such inconsistencies in the data itself produce errors in variables which, using ordinary least squares, lead to biased and inconsistent estimates of the model parameters. A model that incorporates inaccurate data will produce equally inaccurate forecasts.

Every statistical study must cope with the inferior quality of the data. However, as can be seen in Table 4.1 on p. 56, certain studies exacerbate the data problem by unnecessarily truncating their data set. To avoid loss of information on the population, as large a data set as possible must be used for statistical analysis. Model estimates derived from data covering a restrictively short time interval or a narrow geographic area may improve the historical classification efficiency due to the homogeneity of the sample, but will not reflect the true parameters of the much larger total debtor population.

To avoid a restrictively limited data pool, all the studies listed in Table 4.1 have pooled time-series and cross-sectional data. The time horizon of the panel data used in these studies ranged from seven years in the paper by Sargen (1977) to eighteen years in the model by Saini and Bates (1978). The number of countries also varied considerably, ranging from twenty-five (Saini and Bates, 1978) to eighty-one (Dhonte, 1974). As shown in Table 4.1, the number of observations typically is much less than the potential full sample (that is, the product of the number of countries and years) due to missing values. For example, the total number of actual observation points in these studies ranged from 81 to 580, while the number of potential sample points ranged from 328 to 1,053. On average only 62 per cent of the potential observation points in these studies were available due to missing or incomplete data.

If each yearly observation for a particular country is independent from the next year, then pooling the data is acceptable and this will generate an adequate number of observation points to ensure sufficient degrees of freedom in all the listed studies. If the assumption of independence does not hold true, however, and it seems likely that it does not, then the results of several studies become problematical due to insufficient degrees of freedom. None of these studies address the issue of independence of observations either across countries or over time.

The estimation of an individual country rescheduling model is precluded by a small number of rescheduling observations and other time-series data for any particular country. Similarly, cross-sectional estimation is also ruled out owing to an insufficient number of rescheduling observations in any given year. Since country-year observations are probably not independent and identically distributed, the use of panel data or pooled time-series and cross-sectional data requires a fixed-effects econometric specification. This will be discussed in more detail in Chapter 6.

Rescheduling Definition

The interpretation of the rescheduling process and the definition of the binary-valued dependent variable is a third major problem of the debt early warning models. Most of these studies defined a rescheduling as the year in which a multilateral rescheduling agreement was finalized. Negotiation of a debt rescheduling agreement, however, is an extended process which many times is not completed until many months or even years after the onset of debt service payment arrears. Pinpointing a particular rescheduling year to identify what is probably a multi-year process is clearly problematical.

The difficulty of identification is compounded when various creditors (for example, donor governments, financial institutions, etc.) reach agreements with a particular borrower in different years. Presumably, both reschedulings, although occurring in different years, result from the same financial disequilibrium. The best solution to this problem is to identify the rescheduling observation with the onset of arrears. Unfortunately this data typically is not available for all developing countries. Hence an alternative solution must be found.

Since the resource imbalance associated with the debt rescheduling usually persists for several years, the use of successive rescheduling points, starting with the estimated year in which arrears first occurred and ending with the year of the last related debt rescheduling, may be the preferred solution. For prognosticative purposes, the initial year of arrears must be pinpointed since the ultimate purpose of the model is to predict future payments difficulties and adjust the portfolio accordingly before the problems arise.

Successive rescheduling agreements with different creditors may be due to the same external payments imbalance. It is less likely, however, that successive reschedulings by the same creditor occur because of the initial resource imbalance alone. Correlated reschedulings require an additional term in the model specification, whether due to inadequate terms of the prior rescheduling, the debtor's inability to tap global credit supply, or the debtor's unwillingness to adjust resource supply and demand. While none of the studies listed in Table 4.1 addressed this issue, the influence which past rescheduling can have on the likelihood of subsequent reschedulings (that is, rescheduling state dependence) must be measured. This will be addressed in more detail in Chapter 5.

Most of these studies used rescheduling observation points which comprised multilateral reschedulings only. Agreements with other creditors, whether bilateral or private, were usually omitted. Although most bilateral reschedulings involve debt of relatively small magnitudes, they also should be included as rescheduling observations, as should the growing number of private bank debt repayment negotiations.

Saini and Bates (1978) altered the rescheduling definition to include major balance of payments support loans. Such loans, in contrast to arrears, represent an alternative signal of debt servicing problems. Saini and Bates also excluded 'voluntary reschedulings' since these were thought to be more indicative of intended resource transfer rather than acute balance of payments difficulties. The statistical results were measurably improved with the use of this modified dependent variable.

Maroni (1977) and Erbe and Schattner (1980) suggest the inclusion of emergency foreign exchange controls, IMF stabilization programmes, or unsolicited commercial bank refinancings as rescheduling points. Although indicative of a cash-flow squeeze, these alternatives represent policy-response options to debt difficulties which do not necessarily imply immediate costs to lending institutions. Therefore, these definitions are not appropriate for use in a dichotomous univariate model. It may be useful, however, to incorporate a dichotomous interpretation of such adjustment policies in a multivariate discrete choice model, or, alternatively, a nested polychotomous interpretation of these events in a univariate discrete choice model. These possibilities are left for future research.

Multivariate Method
The choice of multivariate method represents a fourth major issue when building a model of rescheduling risk. Numerous multivariate methods could be used to stratify sample data and obtain inferential conclusions about the underlying population. While the preceding studies incorporated either discriminant, principal component or logit regression analysis, Kendall (1975) presents still other statistical techniques which could be utilized. This section will critically review these three multivariate procedures and decide on the method which is most appropriate for modelling sovereign rescheduling risk.

DISCRIMINANT ANALYSIS
Among the credit-scoring models listed in Table 4.1 on p. 56 the statistical procedure used most frequently is discriminant analysis.[4] This method assumes that there are two discrete, mutually exclusive population groups (see Figure 4.1.a). This binary classification is

obtained by a discriminant function constructed as a linear combination of explanatory variables, X_i, and their respective estimated weights, a_i (see Equation 4.1).

$$Y = \sum_{i=1}^{n} a_i X_i$$

Equation 4.1

The coefficients, a_i, are estimated so that the ratio of the sample variance between the two groups to the variance within the two groups is maximized. Next, a Y-value is computed for each point in the pooled data, from which a frequency distribution of Y-values for both groups is obtained. A critical value is determined from the mean Y-values and the assumed cost of both Type I and Type II errors. This critical value is used to differentiate old or new data according to the two population groups.

Despite its wide use in sovereign credit-scoring models, discriminant analysis possesses certain conceptual and statistical deficiencies which represent serious methodological limitations for its application to country-risk analysis.

The standard discriminant analysis procedures assume that the explanatory variables in the estimated function are multivariate normally distributed. In the applied literature the problem of testing for the appropriateness of the distribution has been largely ignored. Moreover, most available normality tests are for univariate not multivariate problems. If the normality hypothesis is rejected, one must face the practically impossible task of deriving the appropriate alternative joint probability density function. Even though it is quite likely that in most cases the normality assumption does not hold, most applications proceed as if it did, and use the standard statistical procedures. The robustness of the test statistics under these circumstances have not been conclusively determined.

A second critical assumption of classical linear discriminant analysis is that the group variance-covariance matrices are equal across all groups. Insufficient theoretical development precludes an adequate testing procedure for this multivariate precondition. It is likely that a sample, particularly a relatively small one, will violate this tenet. Violation of this assumption may affect the reliability of the test for the equality of group means. Moreover, depending upon the two sample sizes, the number of explanatory variables and the differences in their dispersions, use of linear classification rules

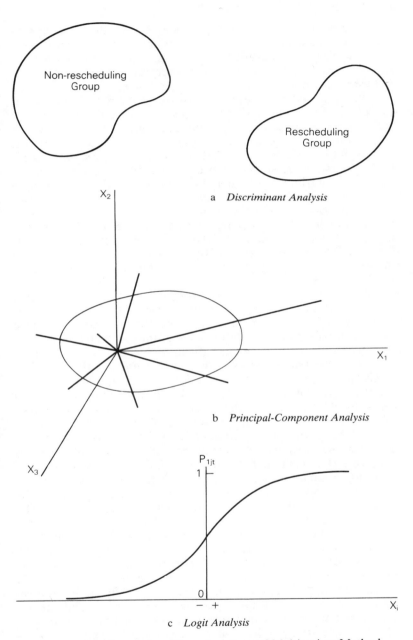

a *Discriminant Analysis*

b *Principal-Component Analysis*

c *Logit Analysis*

Figure 4.1 Population Characteristics and Multivariate Method

when quadratic rules are indicated may distort the classification results. Unequal dispersions (that is, variance-covariance matrices) imply the use of a quadratic function. Use of a non-linear function, however, renders the isolation and interpretation of the effect of individual explanatory variables more complex.

Unlike the coefficients in the classical linear regression model, the discriminant function coefficients are not unique. Only the ratios of the coefficients are unique. Since it is not possible to test whether a particular coefficient in the discriminant function is or is not equal to zero, a test for its individual explanatory significance is also impossible. A step-wise backward method based upon the variable's contribution to the multivariate F statistic can be used to determine the relative importance of variables. However, this method also assumes equal variance-covariance matrices; the violation of which will bias the hypothesis testing. Since classification accuracy is a fundamental goal, the criterion for retaining or deleting a variable should be related to its overall efficiency regarding the classification results, rather than its performance in a standard signficance test.

Discriminant analysis is also restricted in its ability to project a classification scheme into the future. It must be assumed that the basic differences among the means and the variance-covariance matrices for all groups are stationary over the specified time period. Evidence of structural change affecting a debtor's rescheduling probability, obtained in this study and by Saini and Bates (1978), verifies the relevance of this methodological limitation.

Since *a priori* probabilities of the classification of the population are unavailable, some of the studies using discriminant analysis assume that the two groups possess equal probabilities of occurrence. Unless the groups are equally likely to occur, which they probably are not, then the estimated error rates will bear no relationship to what might be expected in the population.

A limited sample size also has been a weakness of these studies. When the two populations are of greatly unequal size, it may be difficult to determine the classification table. Regardless of the magnitude of the total sample, the effective sample size for determining the ability to discriminate is limited by the smaller of the two groups. Were this rule to be followed for the examples listed in Table 4.1 on p. 56, the average effective sample size would be reduced to only 10 per cent of the original pooled sample.

The arbitrary selection of the discriminant function's critical value, which distinguishes between creditworthy and uncreditworthy borrowers, is another serious problem of this technique. Most of these studies select this value without an explicit or systematic reason. Choosing this value so as to minimize the number of total errors in the sample period may produce a satisfying historical classification rate, but could hinder the identification of future rescheduling candidates.

For all these reasons, discriminant analysis is considered to be inappropriate for modelling sovereign rescheduling risk.

PRINCIPAL COMPONENT ANALYSIS

Chronologically, principal component analysis was the second statistical technique applied to the study of sovereign rescheduling risk. Nonetheless, it was used only once (Dhonte, 1974). This technique computes a new set of mutually orthogonal values from a linear combination of the original variables, X_i (see Figure 4.1.b on p. 63). These are defined in Equation 4.2.

$$L_i = a_1X_1 + a_2X_2 + \cdots + a_kX_k,$$
such that:
$$a_1 + a_2 + \cdots + a_k = 1;$$
the variance of (4.2) is maximized; and
the L_i, for all i, are orthogonal.

Equation 4.2

The informational content of each component, L_i, is defined as the sum of squares of distances of plots along that component. This is expressed as a percentage of the sample variance and serves as a measure of the relative importance of each component. The important principal components (that is, those with the most informational content) are retained as uncorrelated independent variables.

Unlike a regression equation, in which the sum of squares is minimized in particular directions, principal component analysis simply minimizes the sum of squares of the distance between the original plot and the components. Therefore, this technique cannot contribute to the inferential causality between the independent variable and the probability of rescheduling. It merely designates the relationships among the independent variables themselves. For example, even though the first principal component will represent the maximum variance of the independent variables, it may not possess the highest correlation with Y, the probability of rescheduling.

Secondly, an acceptable algorithm does not exist for the elimination of superfluous independent variables from the original list. Hence, one is required to resort to an unacceptable trial-and-error process.

An additional problem arises when the independent variables are not measured in identical units. If they are not, it is difficult to interpret such concepts as the total sample variance and to ascribe portions of this variance to each component.

For these reasons, principal component analysis is not appropriate as the main inferential technique for rescheduling-risk modelling. However, it can be a useful aid to understanding the relationships amongst the explanatory variables.

LOGIT AND LINEAR-PROBABILITY REGRESSION ANALYSIS

Regression analysis is the statistical method chosen for use in this study since it is theoretically superior and statistically more robust than either discriminant analysis or principal component analysis when applied to the study of sovereign debt rescheduling risk. From a theoretical perspective, the logit model is the most appealing functional form. Due to several attendant statistical limitations concerning the estimation process, however, the linear probability model will be tested along with the logit model in Chapter 6.[5]

It is likely that the sample countries are drawn from one population which exhibits a whole continuum of abilities to service debt. Thus, it is not theoretically appropriate to divide observation points (that is, country-years) into two mutually exclusive populations according to the countries' prior rescheduling experience, as discriminant analysis necessitates. By contrast, logit analysis presumes only one underlying population and that a rescheduling occurs after the cumulative effect of a number of explanatory variables reaches a critical level. The cumulative density function of the logit function is shown in Figure 4.1.c on p. 63. According to the *a priori* theoretical notion of a sovereign country's debt rescheduling behaviour, the threshold nature of the cumulative logistic density function is preferred to the constant elasticity linear probability model.

Another important advantage of logit analysis over both discriminant and principal component analysis is the robustness of its statistical tests, given less than ideal population characteristics. It has been shown by Efron (1975) that if the population data are multivariate normal with equal dispersion matrices, then discriminant analysis yields better estimates. However, these assumptions are unlikely to be met, even approximately, as will be shown in Chapter 6. Whenever the normality assumptions are violated, Collins and Green (1982) recommend the use of a logit model using a maximum likelihood estimator. Furthermore, unlike the coefficients in discriminant analysis, those in the logit model can be tested individually for significance, allowing a systematic method of variable selection.

In this study, the logit model is estimated using the maximum likelihood method. McFadden (1973) has shown that under quite general conditions, this estimation method produces coefficients which possess desirable properties of consistency, asymptotic efficiency, and asymptotic normality.

Despite the apparent theoretical and operational advantages of logit analysis over both discriminant and principal component analysis, Saini and Bates (1978) found that its retrospective classification efficiency may not always be superior to discriminant analysis. Nonetheless, Smith (1977) presents evidence that logit analysis possesses superior predictive abilities to these other two multivariate methods. Ingram and Frazier (1982) conclude that this is especially true for minimizing Type I error rates, which are clearly of more interest to creditors than Type II errors.

Despite the theoretical advantages of logit analysis, many of the traditional econometric estimation problems cannot easily be dealt with when using a logit model with panel data. For an efficient estimation strategy, Amemiya (1981) recommends the use of a linear probability model as a preliminary step toward a more sophisticated functional form. Therefore, a linear probability model will be initially estimated to obtain preliminary results. As a special case of the standard linear model when the dependent variable is dichotomous, this model allows easy diagnostic testing and can be corrected for violations of the best linear unbiased estimator (BLUE) at minimal computational expense. The estimator for the linear probability model will be tested and adjusted for autocorrelation, heteroscedasticity and a fixed-effects specification.

Econometric Estimation
From the dearth of econometric issues presented in the logit regression studies listed in Table 4.1 on p. 56, the authors tacitly assume that all the basic assumptions of the standard regression model are fulfilled.[6] However, the preceding section has identified several violations of these assumptions which require attention. These statistical problems include: specification error, errors in variables, improper pooling of data, autocorrelation, heteroscedasticity and use of an inappropriate multivariate technique. Chapter 5 and 6 will address these issues in the context of this study's estimation strategy.

End-Chapter Note

1   By implication, it was the smaller banks in the sample which used solely the fully qualitative approach to country risk assessment. Owing to the inadequacies of this method, it is not surprising that many of the smaller regional banks relied more heavily on 'follow the leader' lending practices. In the aggregate, such behaviour would amplify and exaggerate trends in lending activity which could contribute to lending cycles as postulated by Kindleberger, 1981, exhibiting periods of 'euphoria' followed by lending 'revulsion'. Moreover, inadequate credit-scoring techniques may have led the smaller regional banks to underestimate

the actual rescheduling risk of the sovereign debtor, overlending in the 1970s, and ultimately spurn all new lending in an attempt to sharply reduce net exposure once signs of distress were apparent. This 'free-rider' problem greatly exacerbated the debt crisis after August 1982.

2 These statistical studies include Frank and Cline, 1971; Dhonte, 1974; Grinols, 1976; Feder and Just, 1977; Sargen, 1977; Mayo and Barret, 1977; Smith, 1977; and Saini and Bates, 1978. For a representative sample of the earlier heuristic works, see Domar, 1950; Avramovic and Gulhati, 1958; Alter, 1961; Mikesell, 1962; Avramovic, *et al.* 1964; Gulhati, 1967; and Bitterman, 1973.

3 The model presented in Chapter 5 incorporates a measure of the debtor's international price competitiveness (for example, its relative purchasing power parity index). The results of this model (shown in Chapter 6) support Sargen's contention that price disequilibria are an important determinant of debt service capacity. His choice of terminology, however, is unfortunate. Although postulated as defining a country's 'liquidity' rescheduling probability, real exchange rate alignment is part of the debtor's medium-term adjustment capability. In contrast, liquidity reschedulings encompass short-term demand and supply aspects of creditworthiness such as borrowing strategy and debt service roll-over capabilities, respectively.

4 This statistical technique was used by Frank and Cline, 1971; Grinols, 1976; Sargen, 1977; Smith, 1977; and Saini and Bates, 1978.

5 To date, none of the published studies on sovereign debt rescheduling behaviour have used a linear probability model.

6 Feder and Just, 1977; Mayo and Barret, 1977; Smith, 1977; Feder, Just and Ross, 1981; and Cline, 1984 have all used the logit regression technique.

PART III

Country Risk Analysis and Portfolio Management

5.
A Theory of Sovereign Debt Rescheduling Risk

5.1 Introduction

Section 5.2 presents a Lancaster-type theory of consumer choice behaviour applied to sovereign debt rescheduling decisions.[1] It is postulated that debt rescheduling behaviour occurs according to a constrained utility maximization decision-making structure. This microeconomic framework facilitates the selection of explanatory variables for the discrete choice model of debt rescheduling. It also guides the choice of the model's functional form and other empirical considerations such as the estimation technique.

The specification of the model is based equally on the macroeconomic foundations of sovereign creditworthiness. A summary of the relevant macroeconomic theory and the reduced-form econometric specification is presented in section 5.3 of this chapter.

Finally, section 5.4 reviews the statistical properties of two discrete choice (binary valued) probability functions, namely the linear probability and logit models. Based on the statistical properties of these two functional forms, and on the anticipated characteristics of the data base, several different estimators are presented.

5.2 Microeconomic Foundations of Debt Rescheduling Behaviour

The decision to enter the international capital markets as a debtor country rests on the attempt to escape from a low level poverty trap, with the intention of eventually achieving self-sustained growth of per capita real national income. The borrower intends to overcome the initial gaps to growth (for example savings, absorptive capacity, foreign exchange, human capital, or agricultural) by changing the composition of output and increasing domestic savings and foreign exchange earnings to levels which will sustain real growth of per capita income without the use of external funding. This, in turn, permits the net export of capital, and the repayment of foreign debt obligations.

Once the debtor has tapped the international capital markets and accumulated foreign debt obligations, a unique probability exists in any given time period (for example, one year) which represents the country's risk of rescheduling. It is postulated that a debtor country's rescheduling probability is determined by the behavioural process of a rational economic agent (that is, the policy-maker of the debtor country). A Lancaster-type consumption activity utility framework is used to describe this decision-making process.

It is assumed that the individual decision maker (hereinafter termed 'debtor country') possesses a set, **A**, of two mutually exclusive alternative choices concerning external debt management. These two choices are the maintenance of an uninterrupted borrowing process (that is, non-rescheduling), or simply rescheduling.[2]

The non-rescheduling consumption activity comprises actions necessary for successful economic development. For example, it would be a vector which includes credit-financed imported goods and services, fulfilment of investment targets, an increase in real income, drawdown of foreign loans, negotiation for new loan commitments and the repayment of debt service. On the other hand, the rescheduling consumption activity incorporates an alternative strategy which determines a different vector of goods, services and tactical decisions. For example, these components would include fewer purchases of imported goods and services, lower investment levels, a slower growth rate of real income, fewer loan disbursements, severance of commercial credit lines, arrears on debt service payments and even debt repudiation.

Each respective consumption activity vector comprises a unique set of tangible goods, services and tactical decisions (including the rescheduling mode). Each vector imparts an array of qualities or 'degrees of satisfaction' for which an ordinal utility function is defined. Thus, the debtor country can rank the consumption activities within **A** in order of preference. Subject to its given tastes, as well as the economic, financial and political constraints which impinge on the choice set in the characteristic space, the debtor country selects the consumption activity which is most advantageous (that is, maximizes its net derived utility). The vector of goods and tactics associated with the chosen consumption activity defines the observed demands and thus reveals a country's debt rescheduling behaviour.

Let **y** be a finite vector which denotes a specific consumption activity contained in a larger set, **A**. As described above, associated with each **y** is a finite vector of qualities or want satisfaction levels,

$x = Cy$, and a fixed vector of observed attributes, $z = By$. Both C and B represent linear transformations and are assumed to be determined objectively.[3] The debtor country's utility function is defined on these qualities, x, of the consumption activity, y, and also on a vector of country-specific economic, financial and political characteristics, r, which influence taste. Thus, debtor country utility is a function:

$$u_{ijt} = P(x_i, r_j)$$

Where: x_i is a vector of qualities or want satisfaction levels of the ith choice (rescheduling of non-rescheduling);

        r_j is a vector of financial, economic, and political characteristics of the jth debtor country;

        t is the time period, $1, \ldots, T$.

Equation 5.1

The debtor country chooses its borrowing strategy in every period by solving the problem:

$$\text{Max } P(Cy, r)$$
$$a\varepsilon A$$

Equation 5.2

The chosen consumption activity, y^*, determines the debtor country's rescheduling behaviour (that is, observed rescheduling mode demand) through the attributes vector, $z^* = By^*$. If a one-to-one correspondence between attributes and activities is assumed (that is, B is a square, non-singular matrix), then the optimization problem and hence the rescheduling decision can be expressed directly in terms of the observed attributes, z, and the debtor country characteristics, r. Thus, Equation 5.1 is transformed to:

$$u_{ijt} = U(CB^{-1}z, r)$$

Equation 5.3

Now Equation 5.2 can be rewritten as:

$$\text{Max } U(z, r)$$
$$z \ \varepsilon \ By \ \varepsilon \ A$$

Equation 5.4

In this form, the country maximizes over the observed attributes of the choice mode, z, given its tastes and the relevant 'budget constraints' or country specific economic, financial, and political characteristics, r.

However, to make Equation 5.4 operational for empirical application, the structure of rescheduling preferences and its implication for rescheduling risk modelling must be determined. A typical demand function is determined by the relative prices of close substitutes and complements. The cost of other commodity prices are thought to be irrelevant. In a similar manner, it is assumed that the decision to reschedule foreign debt obligations depends only on the attributes of the immediate rescheduling choice mode, as well as those attributes which are close substitutes or complements to this choice mode.

In the context of sovereign debtor behaviour, close substitutes to the rescheduling mode include only the immediate alternative to rescheduling: maintenance of debt-service payments. Close substitutes represent alternative means to accomplish identical or very similar results of long-term development. The tactical choice between rescheduling or non-rescheduling represents a decision between alternative paths to the common goal of self-sustained economic growth and development. In fact, the perceived respective attributes of these close substitutes will primarily determine which outcome is chosen. The other determining factor is the combined attributes of the complementary choices.

Close complements to the debt rescheduling and non-rescheduling choice modes represent additional decisions within the consumption activity vectors. These complementary decisions can either influence or be influenced by the rescheduling decision itself. For example, when the rescheduling mode is chosen, the country is likely to be denied adequate access to new foreign credit. This will force a reduction or reorientation of its foreign trade activity (for example, reduced imports, or increased counter trade) which could force a change in development strategy. Hence, choosing the rescheduling mode requires an implicit decision concerning the amount of foreign credit required by the desired development strategy. In this case, the complementary decision is affected by the choice of rescheduling versus non-rescheduling.

Complementary decisions can also influence rescheduling probability. The inability or the unwillingness to implement an adequate stabilization programme will deplete foreign exchange reserves, accelerate borrowing needs, and diminish externally perceived creditworthiness. This, in turn, limits the external financing options and increases the likelihood of the rescheduling choice mode. Hence, prior decisions concerning trade and external financial policy can directly affect the choice between the rescheduling and non-rescheduling choice modes.

Choosing a manageable number of close substitutes and complements for the econometric specification requires an underlying assumption on the separability of preferences.[4] The complexity of the estimation problem is diminished significantly by factoring the demand function into its component decisions. These concern the choice of: the rescheduling versus the non-rescheduling mode, short-term preference for international liquidity, medium-term demand management policies and long-term development strategy. Assume a decision sequence involving the choices shown in Figure 5.1. Policy-makers first choose to pursue the transformation of their country from a low-income agricultural economy to an industrial power. Next, a decision is made concerning the development strategy and the domestic versus foreign composition of gross

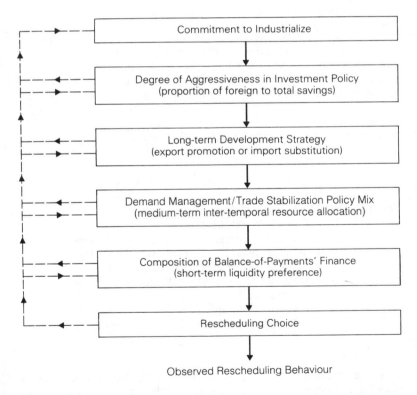

Figure 5.1 Decision Sequence of the Consumption Activity Vector

national savings (that is, the aggressiveness of the investment programme and external debt accumulation). This is followed by the choice of demand management policy, external financial management, and finally the rescheduling mode itself.

At each stage of decision making, the choice is conditioned on both the prior decision path as well as the preferred sebsequent outcome. The solid lines indicate the decision sequence. The dotted lines represent the information flows that enter each decision level and affect the optimality of sequential choices.

With the assumption of a separable utility function, an indicator representing the utility or disutility of succeeding choices is sufficient information at each decision level. Thus, a fully specified model of debt rescheduling behaviour necessarily includes, at each decision level, indicators representing information from succeeding choices. Since this flow of information, involving substitute and complementary choice attributes, is incorporated in the utility maximization process of Equation 5.4, the decision model is stated directly in utility terms.

In the ultimate decision stage as outlined in Figure 5.1, the jth debtor country in the population faces only I alternatives indexed $i=[0,1]$. These two choice modes represent non-rescheduling and rescheduling, respectively. Each alternative mode has a vector of observed attributes, z_i. The debtor country possesses a utility function identical to that described in Equation 5.3 which varies over the population. This variation is the result of a vector of unobserved or unmeasured choice attributes or country-specific characteristics, ε_{ij}. Thus, Equation 5.3 is rewritten to include this stochastic element:

$$u_{ijt} = V(z_i, r_j) + \varepsilon_{ij}$$

Where: V is non-stochastic and expresses the average tastes of the population;

   ε_{ij} is a random variable with a mean independent of z and reflects unmeasured country-specific tastes or choice mode attributes;

   z_i is a vector of the observed attributes of the ith choice; and

   r_j is a vector of financial, economic, and political characteristics of the jth debtor country.

Equation 5.5

In every decision period (that is, one year), the debtor country chooses the consumption activity vector that maximizes its utility and thus determines the rescheduling mode. In particular, this decision is based on the maximization of the utility associated with the attributes of the rescheduling choice modes. This maximization process is subject to the 'budget constraints' or the characteristics of the complementary choices at each level in the activity vector decision sequence. With this structure, the jth debtor country will choose to reschedule its foreign debt payments only when:

$$V_t(z_1, r_j) + \varepsilon_{1j} > V_t(z_0, r_j) + \varepsilon_{0j}$$
for each j and all t.

Equation 5.6

Note that since z_0 and z_1 are continuous random variables, indecision (that is, $V_{0jt} = V_{1jt}$; for all j,t) will occur with zero probability. Also, because of the stochastic nature of Equation 5.6, an individual debtor country drawn at random from the population will choose to reschedule with probability, P. So Equation 5.6 becomes:

$$P_{1jt}(\theta, z, r) = \text{Prob} \; (\varepsilon_{0j} - \varepsilon_{1j} < V_{1t} - V_{0t})$$
for each j and all t.

Equation 5.7

A simple rearrangement of terms yields:

$$P_{1jt}(\theta, z, r) = \text{Prob} \left(\frac{V_1 - V_0}{\sigma} > \frac{\mu}{\sigma} \right) \text{ for each j and all t}$$

Where: $\mu = (\varepsilon_{0j} - \varepsilon_{1j})$; and
$\sigma = $ the standard deviation of the error term.[5]

Equation 5.8

Define the cumulative distribution function $F(\cdot)$ as the difference of the stochastic components, $(\varepsilon_{0j} - \varepsilon_{1j})$. Then rewrite Equation 5.8 as:

$$P_{1jt}(\theta, z, r) = F(V_1(z_1, r_j) - V_0(z_0, r_j))$$
for each j and all t.

Equation 5.9

If it is assumed that V is a linear function of the parameters, θ, then Equation 5.9 becomes:

$$P_{1jt} = F(\eta_1(z, r) \beta_1 + \cdots + \eta_k(z, r) \beta_k)$$

where: $\eta_k(z,$ are empirical functions with known
$\quad\quad\quad$ r)$\quad$ parameters.

Equation 5.10

In more compact notation Equation 5.10 becomes:

$$P_{1jt} = F(\eta'\beta)$$

Where:$\quad\quad\eta' = (\eta_1, \ldots, \eta_k)$ is a row vector of
$\quad\quad\quad\quad\quad\quad\quad$ functions; and
$\quad\quad\quad\quad\beta = (\beta_1, \ldots, \beta_k)'$ is a column vector of
$\quad\quad\quad\quad\quad\quad\quad$ unknown parameters.

Equation 5.11

Assume the cumulative density function for the difference of the error
terms is represented by the logistic distribution, so that the *ex ante*
probability of rescheduling is now restated from Equation 5.11 as:

$$P_{1jt}(\beta,\eta) = F\left(\frac{V_1-V_0}{\sigma}\right) = \int_{-\infty}^{\frac{V_1-V_0}{\sigma}} \frac{1}{1+\exp(\eta'\beta)} \quad \text{for all } t$$

Equation 5.12

Thus, the probability of the jth debtor in the time period t demanding a sovereign debt rescheduling is represented by the unshaded
portion of the weibull probability distribution in Figure 5.2.[6]

This microeconomic behavioural model states that debt
rescheduling risk is a function of the observed attributes of the
rescheduling choice modes, z_i, and the 'budget constraints' or
country-specific characteristics of the relevant complementary decisions, r_j. In order to construct these functions, $\eta_k(z, r)$, which
specify rescheduling demand in Equation 5.11, a macroeconomic
theory of sovereign debt service capacity is required.

5.3   Macroeconomic Foundations of Debt Service Capacity

In a Lancaster-type characteristic space, an agent (debtor country)
derives satisfaction from the attributes of the goods, services and
tactical decisions included in a particular consumption activity
rather than from the goods themselves. Thus, formulating a
borrowing strategy is a matter of choosing amongst the available

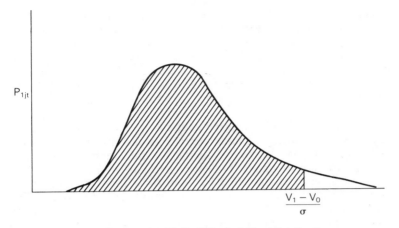

Figure 5.2 The Weibull Probability Distribution

consumption activity vectors within the context of constrained utility maximization. The activity vectors include the observed attributes of the respective rescheduling-mode choices and the characteristics of the other complementary decisions. These factors are the inputs into the debtor country's decision-making process. Once the optimal consumption vector is chosen, the observed (or derived) demand for rescheduling behaviour, development strategy, stabilization policy and debt management occur as the output. Conceptually, the agent maximizes the utility of the rescheduling choice-mode attributes, subject to the three 'budget constraints' or complementary decisions affecting debt service capacity.

Despite the complexity of this decision-making process, the assumed separability of the utility function means that one variable from each level of the postulated decision process (as shown in Figure 5.1 on p. 75), is sufficient to specify the model. Thus, for the rescheduling demand model to capture this behavioural process, the explanatory variables must include the two rescheduling choice-mode attributes, the three identified foreign exchange 'budget constraints' to debt service capacity, and a proxy variable representing the creditor's willingness to lend. Only by the inclusion of all these relevant indicators will the rescheduling model avoid specification bias. Since the explanatory indicators include the cost of borrowing and debtor country policy variables, the estimated model can measure the 'price' elasticity of demand for debt rescheduling, given a change in either external credit terms or in the debtor's policy response to external disturbances.

The vector of attributes, z_i, in Equation 5.10 measures the cost to the debtor country associated with each of the two rescheduling modes. It is postulated that the primary *cost of non-rescheduling* is the necessity to honour scheduled debt service payments. Alternatively, the fundamental *cost of rescheduling* is the ensuing reduced access to external capital markets, resulting in foregone credit-based non-compressible imports, and thus a retardation of the development plan.[7]

The second group of required explanatory variables include the characteristics of the complementary decisions or the foreign exchange 'budget constraints' to the maximization process. The relevant foreign exchange 'budget constraints' to a country's debt service capacity are specified by identifying the determinants or origins of the balance of payments disequilibrium and categorizing these factors according to their shock impact time or their policy response time. These variables are constraints in that they influence the magnitude of the external disequilibrium, change the debtor's net borrowing requirements and thus alter the effective zone in the utility characteristic space.

This classification identifies three temporally distinct groups of variables. When any one of these three constraints is binding, it will contribute a foreign exchange borrowing requirement. Otherwise, the potential constraint is non-binding and contributes a net repayment source. These three foreign exchange 'budget constraints' are: (1) long-term structural variables, (2) medium-term adjustment factors, and (3) short-term liquidity management. These constraints are incorporated into the model as country characteristics which, by their complementary role in the decision-making sequence, indirectly influence the propensity to reschedule. These indicators are either predetermined debtor-country policy variables or exogenous global economic disturbances.

Combined with the need to identify the demand function for debt rescheduling (which is emphasized in this study) it is, of course, necessary for the econometric specification to postulate an explanatory variable which represents the supply function. The cumulative sum of the dependent variable (that is, observed rescheduling behaviour) is used in the empirical portion of this study. A country's past rescheduling experience (rescheduling state dependence) clearly affects the capital market's assessment of sovereign creditworthiness which, in turn, significantly determines the commercial banks' willingness to lend. Sufficient access to continuous external capital disbursements or the banks' willingness to lend is a crucial aspect of short-term creditworthiness.

In its most general form, it is postulated that a country's demand for rescheduling must include the following components:

P_{1jt} = F[rescheduling cost, non-rescheduling cost, rescheduling state dependence, foreign exchange income constraints (liquidity, adjustment and structural)]

Equation 5.13

The rest of this chapter will define these components more precisely, incorporate them into Equation 5.12 and present appropriate estimators for the two alternative functional forms (that is, logit and linear probability models).

Attributes of the Rescheduling Choice Modes

RESCHEDULING COST
It has been assumed that a low-income country borrows funds from abroad to supplement its gross domestic savings and accelerate its development plan. Thus, borrowed funds increase essential imports of goods and services which, if properly used, will expand the debtor's capital stock, raise real GDP growth and accelerate the structural transformation of the economy. Successful long-term structural transformation of the economy will eventually eliminate the need for foreign capital and establish the ability to service the resultant outstanding external liabilities. Were a country to request a unilateral rescheduling, diminished access to external credit or even a concerted international credit embargo is likely to ensue. These prospects for a credit embargo should act as an effective disincentive to such behaviour, given the crucial role of credit financed imports.

The absence of new loan commitments and disbursements would force merchandise imports to a level which could be financed only by current export receipts or foreign exchange reserve usage. If this foreign credit stringency forced the reduction of non-compressible as well as compressible imports, then the costs borne by the debtor would rise even further. Production bottlenecks, rising excess capacity, a higher incremental capital output ratio and employment loss would all contribute to slower GDP growth, a reduction of living standards and diminished long-term creditworthiness.

According to the preceding logic, a debtor country's ratio of import expenditures to GDP indicates the opportunity cost of rescheduling since it measures the country's vulnerability to an international credit embargo. Hence, this ratio is negatively correlated with a debtor's proclivity toward a debt rescheduling. A high level of imports represents a greater cost of rescheduling and thus increases the disincentive to request a debt rescheduling. On the other hand, a low ratio of imports to GDP reflects a more autarchic development strategy which lowers the cost arising from a debt rescheduling request. The incentive to demand a debt rescheduling rises as a country's dependence on credit-based non-compressible imports falls.

It is assumed that the debtor country formulates its decision-making concerning current debt rescheduling behaviour based upon, inter alia, its ratio of imports to GDP in the prior period. Thus, this indicator is lagged one year vis-à-vis the rescheduling observation and represents a predetermined debtor country policy variable.[8]

NON-RESCHEDULING COST

The only alternative to the rescheduling choice mode is the non-rescheduling or sustainable borrowing option. Since uninterrupted external credit access requires the debtor to honour its current debt service obligations, the cost of the non-rescheduling choice mode (or sustainable borrowing) is the current and prospective payments required to service the external debt. The *current* cost of non-rescheduling is measured by the contractual debt service ratio (or the ratio of originally scheduled amortization and interest payments to total export receipts of goods and services). As the cost of the non-rescheduling choice mode rises directly with the debt service ratio, it is positively correlated with the probability of rescheduling.

The *prospective* cost of the non-rescheduling choice mode is the cost of new borrowing. The private grant element of new loan commitments measures the present value of the future net financial transfer as a proportion of total private commercial bank commitments. A higher value signifies a greater real resource transfer and thus a lower cost of borrowing (or cost of non-rescheduling). Hence, rational economic behaviour would dictate a negative relationship between the private grant element and rescheduling probability.

The composite indicator for the cost of non-rescheduling comprises these two variables: a current and prospective price for sustaining the borrowing process. This non-rescheduling cost variable is computed as the difference between the debt service ratio and the private grant element. Thus, the cost of the non-rescheduling choice mode is postulated to be positively correlated with the probability of rescheduling.

Based on the comparison of the respective attribute values (that is, 'prices') of the rescheduling and non-rescheduling choice modes, inter alia, the debtor country formulates its rescheduling behaviour. The explanatory variable representing the non-rescheduling choice mode is specified contemporaneously vis-à-vis the rescheduling observation. These two choice mode 'prices' or attributes represent either predetermined debtor country policy variables or exogenously determined random variables.[9]

Debtor Country Characteristics for Debt Service Capacity
In the determination of debt-rescheduling demand, debtor country characteristics, r_j, are assumed to represent foreign exchange 'budget constraints' to sustained growth of debtor country output. These budget constraints are defined by identifying the causes or origins of a balance of payments disequilibrium. Next, the best respective policy response or adjustment mechanism to alleviate these constraints is identified and categorized according to its impact time lag.[10] By categorizing the response time of balance of payments policy variables and the disturbance impact time of external economic variables as they affect a country's external accounts, three temporally distinct foreign exchange constraints to debt service capacity are identified. These constraints are: (1) long-term structural variables, (2) medium-term adjustment factors, and (3) short-term liquidity management. Depending upon the values of the determinant variables, each of these constraints separately will result in either a foreign borrowing requirement or a net repayment source.

Sustained creditworthiness not only demands that repayment sources equal or exceed borrowing requirements, but also that the source of repayment systematically shifts from external borrowing to internally generated surplus resources. In this manner, a country will maintain a balance between foreign exchange asset liability flow in every period, while it secularly reduces and eventually eliminates its net borrowing requirements.

These foreign exchange income constraints comprise separate determinant variables as follows:

structural constraints   = S (saving rate behaviour, investment and absorptive capacity, foreign trade elasticities, terms of trade)

Equation 5.14

adjustment constraints = A (open-economy demand-management policies, cost and price structures, global trade trends)

Equation 5.15

liquidity constraints   = L (debt terms, debt level, international reserve pool, capital
access)

Equation 5.16

The structural constraint is determined by the debtor country's ability to mobilize a sufficient domestic surplus over and above consumption (saving capacity), efficiently transform a portion of these resources into productive capital stock capable of producing potentially tradeable goods (investment and absorptive capacity) and convert the balance of the domestic surplus into foreign exchange without decreasing its international unit value (foreign exchange capacity). In this manner, the export-based import capacity is increased which removes the foreign exchange gap to growth. When any one of three structural gaps (for example, savings, absorptive capacity, and foreign exchange) or others are binding, growth of per capita output will be limited and the economy's long-term creditworthiness diminished. The incremental capital-output ratio is chosen as the best proxy explanatory variable for this complex structural process.[11]

Timely and effective implementation of trade adjustment policies in response to disturbances transmitted by means of the balance of payments is the fundamental condition for a debtor country to maintain its medium-term debt service capacity. The source of these disturbances may be either internally or externally generated and their effect may be transmitted through either the current or capital external account. The range of policy options will be partially circumscribed by the state of the structural constraints of the economy (for example, degree of import compressibility, income elasticity of export supply, price and income elasticity of export demand and terms of trade trends). Nonetheless, adjustment policies must ensure the timely elimination of the cyclically induced portion of the external disequilibrium, thereby lowering gross borrowing requirements. The relative purchasing power parity index is the chosen proxy explanatory variable for this disturbance-stabilization or adjustment aspect of creditworthiness.[12]

A debtor must actively manage its external financial policy in order to maintain its short-term creditworthiness. In the early stages of the growth-cum-indebtedness process, a positive net financial transfer is required to finance the binding long-term and medium-term constraints to creditworthiness. Since it will take some time to eliminate these longer term net borrowing requirements, short-term debt management must ensure that external capital flows supply a net repayment source (that is, a positive net financial transfer) for an extended and uninterrupted period of time. Prudence is required, however, so that the stock dependence (debt level) and the flow dependence (net financial transfer) do not become excessive.[13] Rapid debt accumulation can diminish externally perceived creditworthiness and reduce access to new foreign capital, thus tightening the liquidity constraint. Hence, external financial policy must ensure that the stock and flow dependence on foreign debt, combined with the terms of debt repayment, do not interrupt the roll-over process. If amortization payments on external debt cannot be refinanced (that is, rolled over), then the liquidity constraint is binding. In this case, the supply of new financial asset flows (for example, loan disbursements and international reserves) is inadequate. The ratio of disbursed debt to international reserves is the explanatory variable chosen to represent the liquidity constraint.[14]

Dynamics of Demand for Debt Rescheduling
The ratio of non-compressible (or essential) imports to total imports (NCM) is the theoretically preferred attribute value or price of the rescheduling choice mode.[15] The price or attribute value of the non-rescheduling choice mode is represented by a composite variable comprising scheduled debt-service payments and the private grant element. As such, the non-rescheduling choice mode or price of debt service (DSC) comprises both the current and the prospective costs associated with sustainable borrowing. These attributes of the respective choice modes (NCM and DSC) define the two axes in Figure 5.3

A change in the value of either choice-mode attribute directly affects the rescheduling probability by altering the relative utility (and thus the ranking) of the consumption activity vectors. For a given set of choice-mode vectors, r_1 and nr_1, either an increase in the DSC or a decline in NCM will increase the probability of rescheduling, by skewing the utility space toward the rescheduling choice-mode vector, r_1.

The relative position of the rescheduling vector, r_1, and non-rescheduling vector, nr_1, within the quadrant are determined by the values of the economic characteristics or 'budget constraints'. Thus changes in the values of this set of predetermined or exogenously determined financial and economic characteristics of the debtor country, indirectly affect the rescheduling probability by shifting the pair of vectors relative to the choice mode attributes. Thus, prior economic policy decisions or balance of payments disturbances which tighten the budget constraints will shift the r_1 and nr_1 vectors clockwise. For a given set of attribute costs (that is, DSC and NCM), this clockwise shift of the two vectors represents a

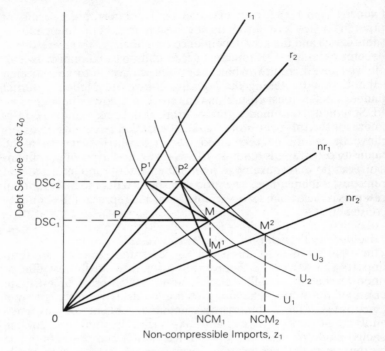

Figure 5.3   Activity Vector Optimization in Characteristic Space

tightening of the foreign exchange budget constraint, thus increasing the probability of rescheduling.

For example, assume that the initial ratio of non-compressible imports is at NCM_1, the debt service cost is represented by DSC_1, and the rescheduling and non-rescheduling consumption vectors are shown by r_1 and nr_1, respectively. Within this delimited characteristic space, OPM, the optimal point is found at M since the debtor reaches U_2, the indifference curve representing the highest achievable utility. This implies a derived demand for the non-rescheduling choice mode since M falls directly on the non-rescheduling vector, nr_1.

While non-compressible imports remain at the same level, NCM_1, assume that debt service cost rises to DSC_2 due to either an increase in LIBOR (which raises debt service payments) or to a decline in perceived creditworthiness (which increases the price of new borrowing). As a result, the characteristic space has been enlarged to OP^1M and is now more skewed toward the rescheduling vector. This is intuitively plausible since the new attribute value or cost of the non-rescheduling choice mode, DSC_2, has risen. Despite this increase in the probability of rescheduling, the optimal activity vector remains at M, implying continued sustainable borrowing. This new higher level of rescheduling probability reflects the fact that the higher DSC value makes the country more susceptible to adversely shifting budget constraints. For example, while NCM_1 and DSC_2 remain at their respective levels, assume a tightened budget constraint due to a decline in the country's marginal efficiency of investment. This decline in long-term creditworthiness shifts the consumption vectors clockwise from r_1 and nr_1 to r_2 and nr_2, respectively. Given the new characteristic space, OP^2M^1, utility is maximized at P^2. This optimal point would result in a rescheduling request since it lies on the rescheduling activity vector, r_2.

Finally, with the new consumption vectors, r_2 and nr_2, and a level of debt service payments at DSC_2, assume non-compressible imports rise to NCM_2. Despite the tightened budget constraints, the rise in the attribute value of rescheduling to NCM_2 is sufficient to deter a rescheduling request. In the new characteristic space, OP^2M^2, the non-rescheduling consumption activity vector, nr_2, intersects the optimal point M^2, which implies a derived demand for sustained borrowing (that is, non-rescheduling).

By maximizing the perceived utility of the various consumption activity vectors in every time period, the preferred borrowing policy is derived through the choice of the optimal bundle of activities. As has been shown, the optimal activity vector is also affected by the three country characteristics or foreign exchange 'budget constraints' which represent complementary decisions in the choice sequence.

The structural constraint is relaxed (that is, vectors r_1 and nr_1 shift counter clockwise) when development policy alters structural parameters which narrow the binding long-term gaps (for example, savings-investment, foreign-exchange, etc.) and thus lower the external borrowing requirement. To improve long-term creditworthiness, the development strategy must ensure the mobilization of an internally generated surplus of potentially tradeable resources and facilitate the ability to convert this surplus into foreign exchange without experiencing a terms of trade loss.

The medium-term constraint is tightened (vectors r_1 and nr_1 shift clockwise) when either an internally generated disturbance or changes in global markets widen the debtor's current account or overall balance deficit. Prompt and effective adjustment policies in response to these balance of payments shocks would reverse the shift in the consumption vectors, improve medium-term creditworthiness and lower the probability of rescheduling.

Successful financial management includes: (1) continuous access to new disbursements, (2) a stable roll-over process, (3) a net inward transfer to finance development projects and other intertemporal allocation decisions, (4) accumulation of an international reserve buffer, and (5) a smooth debt maturity profile. In contrast, the liquidity constraint is tightened (vectors r_1 and nr_1 move clockwise) when either debt involvement (stock or flow dependence) or the terms of debt repayment interrupt the roll-over process as signified by either insufficient capital disbursements or inadequate international reserves.

Any one of these three budget constraints could be sufficiently stringent to limit foreign exchange manoeuverability, precipitate arrears and increase the likelihood of debt rescheduling. For example, the marginal saving rate may be high and rising while demand management policies imply a sustainable balance between output and absorption. Nonetheless, a short-term *liquidity constraint* – due to either insufficient past savings of foreign exchange, an abrupt cessation of new capital inflows, or higher debt terms – could disrupt the roll-over process and result in rescheduling.

Alternatively, despite the absence of a binding short-term or long-term constraint, an unsustainable medium-term borrowing requirement could result from excess domestic demand or an external disturbance. The tightened *adjustment constraint, ceteris paribus*, increases the probability of a rescheduling request.

Finally, assume that neither the short-term nor medium-term constraints are binding. Nonetheless, a low level of gross domestic savings, coupled with a stagnant marginal saving rate, precludes a narrowing of the long-term borrowing requirement. This would trap the country in a 'long-haul' *structural constraint*, implying continued debt accumulation and eventual debt rescheduling or even repudiation.

Mismanagement of the policies embodied in these three constraints (for example, bad development strategy, inadequate trade adjustment or stabilization policies, or lax debt controls) will result in declining market confidence. This, in turn, will produce a narrower range of policy response options (that is, characteristic space choice set skewed toward rescheduling, r_1), potentially resulting in arrears, and a rescheduling request. Alternatively, astute management of the three constraints over time will normally maintain capital-market confidence and sustained capital access. This will supply adequate debtor country foreign exchange liquidity which, if properly used, would ensure long-term solvency. Eventual structural transformation of the economy would sustain real income growth without the need for foreign savings, thus lowering debt rescheduling risk (see Table 5.1).

Table 5.1 Stylized Dynamics of the Budget Constraint to Debt Rescheduling Demand

Investment stage / Potential budget constraints	Virtual autarchy	Growth-cum-indebtedness initiated	Investment promotion continues; classic boom economy	Gestation period of some investments completed	Investment boom completed	Newly industrialized net capital exporting economy
Short-term liquidity	N or RS (small): No debt or debt service; no borrowing; foreign aid flows only contribute to reserves.	RS: Rapid debt accumulation; debt service is 'capitalized' by roll-over; net transfer is positive; reserves fall.	RS: External debt accumulation still rapid; debt service is fully capitalized by roll-over; net transfer positive and reserves are thin.	RS: External debt accumulation is slower; debt amortization only is capitalized by roll-over; net transfer < 0; net capital flow > 0.	BR: Debt level peaks; net capital flow equals zero; net financial transfer is negative; reserves increase.	BR: Debt reduction; net capital outflow; negative net financial transfer; strong international reserves.
Medium-term adjustment	N or BR (small): Low income and low material expectations result in a small and manageable demand for compressible imports.	N or BR (small): Growing material expectations; compressible imports still low, however; vulnerable to balance of trade supply shocks.	BR: High material expectations; compressible import demand is contained with difficulty; very vulnerable to BOP disturbances.	BR (smaller): Strict trade adjustment policy required to neutralize effect of income growth and consumerism on balance of payments.	N: IMF-style austerity results in expenditure reduction and expenditure switching of compressible imports.	BR: Strong exports and lifting of the long-term structural constraint allows import liberalization, and removal of austerity
Long-term structural	N: Subsistence economy; virtual autarchy; non-compressible imports = food and raw materials only; income inelastic export supply.	BR: Nascent industry; first-stage import substitution or export promotion; non-compressible imports = food, raw materials and investment goods.	BR: Growth quickens; first signs of heavy industry; non-compressible imports = food, raw materials and investment goods; Low price and high income elasticity of import demand.	BR (smaller): Many projects on line; export supply more elastic; higher price and lower income elasticity of import demand; non-compressible imports = food and raw materials.	RS: Major investment projects complete improving export diversity and terms of trade; non-compressible imports = food and raw materials; export surplus > interest payments.	RS: Strong export and import substitution industries result in large net export surplus which finances debt service and new international assets.

Notes: BR: net borrowing requirement.
RS: net repayment source.
N: neutral balance of payments impact; neither a borrowing requirement nor a repayment source.

The key to sustainable borrowing (that is, sovereign credit-worthiness) is to match the binding constraints (borrowing requirements) with the non-binding constraints (net repayment sources) in every decision period. This requires active foreign exchange asset and liability management, whereby the *ex post* net financial transfer meets or exceeds the *ex post* structural and adjustment resource constraints. Sustained creditworthiness requires that the capital inflow hastens the structural transformation of the economy, ultimately leading to the closing of the long-term gaps while maintaining compressible import borrowing requirements near zero. At that juncture, the long-term constraint is transformed into the primary repayment source, offsetting the medium-term borrowing requirement (net compressible import surplus) and the short-term borrowing requirement (net debt repayment).

Section 5.2 presented a univariate dichotomous probability function in order to underpin the microeconomic foundations of sovereign debt rescheduling behaviour. As just outlined, the full specification of the econometric debt model also depends on the macroeconomic determinants of sovereign debt service capacity. Thus, the demand-side behavioural model must include these five functions comprising the choice-mode attributes for the two rescheduling options and the three temporally distinct debtor country characteristics (that is, structural, adjustment and liquidity constraints). As explained in section 5.3, a supply-side proxy variable (rescheduling state dependence) is also required in the model. In order to link these theoretical relationships to an empirical model of sovereign rescheduling demand, the functional form (whether logit, probit, or linear probability) and the estimator for the discrete choice credit scoring model must be chosen. These issues are addressed in section 5.4.

5.4   Discrete-Choice Probability Functions and Estimation Methods

Once a country has tapped the international credit markets and accumulated significant foreign liabilities, a unique probability exists in every time period which represents the risk of cross-border debt rescheduling. In order to construct a precise uni-dimensional ranking of two or more debtor countries according to their financial creditworthiness, this *a priori* probability of rescheduling, P, must be known. Since this probability cannot be observed, however, define a binary variable, Y_{jt}, such that:

$$Y_{jt} = \begin{cases} 0 & \text{non-rescheduling choice-mode occurs with prob-} \\ & \text{ability, } (1\text{-}P_n); \\ 1 & \text{rescheduling choice-mode occurs with probability, } P_n \end{cases}$$

for each country j, where $j = 1, \ldots, J$; and
in each period, t, where $t = 1, \ldots, T$.

Equation 5.17

Assigning a 1 to a rescheduling observation (that is, country-year) and a 0 to a non-rescheduling observation, as specified in Equation 5.17, creates this proxy dependent variable. This observed debt behaviour can be regressed upon the postulated explanatory variables to estimate the unknown parameters and calibrate the demand model. Two separate binary-valued probabilistic choice models are tested, namely the linear and logit probability models. The respective estimators are presented here.

The Linear Probability Model
On the assumption that the cumulative distribution function, $F(\cdot)$, is uniform, then the model shown in Equation 5.11 can be expressed as:

$$P_{jt} = \begin{cases} 0 & \text{when} & \eta'\beta < 0; \\ 1 & \text{when} & \eta'\beta > 1; \\ \eta'\beta & \text{when } 0 \leqslant \eta'\beta \leqslant 1. \end{cases}$$

Equation 5.18

Equation 5.18 corresponds to the truncated linear probability model shown in Figure 5.4a. With this model, the elasticity of rescheduling probability with respect to the explanatory variables (that is, β), is constant over the interval of the response function which does not take on extreme values. Thus, there is no threshold or critical point where rescheduling probability is especially sensitive to changing values of the economic budget constraints, choice-mode attributes, or state dependence.

According to this formulation, the regression equation is:

$$Y_{jt} = \alpha + \eta'\beta + \phi$$

where: Y_{jt} is a random vector of the quantal variable;
η is a matrix of known parameters (explanatory variables measured without error);
β is a vector of unknown parameters;

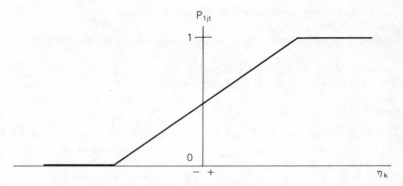

1.   *Truncated Linear Cumulative Density Function*

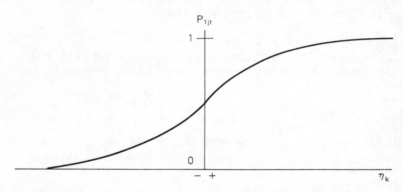

2.   *Logistic Cumulative Density Function*

Figure 5.4   Binary-Valued Cumulative Probability Distribution
Functions

ϕ   is a vector of stochastic disturbance terms
with zero mean;
α   is an unknown scalar vector.

Equation 5.19

From Equations 5.17 and 5.19, it is clear that P measures the
probability that $\varepsilon = 1 - \alpha - \eta'\beta$. It follows that $E(\phi) = 0$ and
$E(\phi^2) = P(1-P)$. Assuming that the sample observations do not take
on extreme values, ordinary least squares will produce unbiased,

and in general consistent, estimators.[16] However, since the variance of ϕ will depend upon the value of P (which, in turn, varies across observations), the error variances will be heteroscedastic and the ordinary least squares estimator will be inefficient.

Assuming that the **Y** values are independent, then the off-diagonal terms of the variance-covariance (that is, dispersion) matrix are zero. In this case, Goldberger (1964) recommends weighted least squares to obtain an efficient estimator for a large sample. The new estimator becomes: $\beta = (X'\hat{U}^{-1}X)^{-1}X'\hat{U}^{-1}Y$, where:

$$U^{-1} = \begin{bmatrix} \dfrac{1}{\hat{Y}_1(1-\hat{Y}_1)} & 0 & . & . & . & 0 \\ 0 & & & & & \\ & & & & & \\ & & & & & 0 \\ & & & & & \\ 0 & . & . & . & 0 & \dfrac{1}{\hat{Y}_n(1-\hat{Y}_n)} \end{bmatrix}$$

Equation 5.20

If the values of $\hat{Y}$ lie outside the unit interval, however, negative variances for the $\hat{U}^{-1}$ matrix in Equation 5.20 will be obtained. This would necessitate dropping these observations from the sample or restricting $\hat{Y}$ to the unit interval. In either case, the weighted least squares estimator is no longer guaranteed to be more efficient than ordinary least squares due to these sample characteristics. Moreover, since $E(\phi^2)$ will be smallest for observations with probabilities close to either one or zero, excessive weight will be placed on extreme observations. Thus, the weighted least squares estimator also magnifies specification error. For these reasons, Domencich and McFadden (1975) suggest use of the ordinary least squares estimator.

Despite the Bernoulli form of the regression error, normal-based test statistics are justified by the asymptotic central-limit theorem and the large sample size of this particular study.

Another problem arising from the statistical nature of the linear probability model concerns its use in prediction. Since $E(\hat{Y}_i/X_i)$ is interpreted as a probability, values outside the [0,1] interval (which could occur due to normal sampling effects) are inconsistent with the restrictions in Equation 5.18. Although setting extreme values equal to zero or one would maintain the probabilistic interpretation of $\hat{Y}$, the predictions would be biased. If Equation 5.19 is estimated using ordinary least squares with the additional constraint, $0 \leqslant \eta' \beta \leqslant 1$, then the estimator will be consistent and more efficient, although biased. For this reason, Pindyck and Rubinfeld (1981) also prefer the ordinary least squares estimator.

There is no ideal estimator for the linear probability model when pooled cross-section and time-series data are used. Ordinary least squares, weighted least squares, and quadratic programming procedures all have certain strengths and weaknesses in this context. As a result, the linear probability model is estimated using three different estimation techniques: (1) ordinary least squares, (2) weighted least squares, and (3) a fixed-effects specification. These estimators address the problems arising from heteroscedasticity and data pooling. The classification efficiency of each model estimator will be presented in Chapter 6.

The Logit Probability Model
In contrast to the linear probability model, assume that the cumulative density function of the difference of the error terms in Equation 5.11 is represented by the logistic distribution. As a result, the logit probability model is obtained:

$$P_{jt} = \frac{1}{1 + \exp(\beta_0 + \beta_1 \eta_1 + \cdots + \beta_k \eta_k)} \quad \text{for all } t$$

Equation 5.21

Equation 5.21 generates the cumulative logistic density function which maps $P(\eta'\beta)$ into the [0,1] interval as shown in Figure 5.4.2. This functional form exhibits a threshold property that is more appealing theoretically than the constant partial rescheduling probability elasticities of the linear probability model. Moreover, since its slope is greatest when $P = 0.5$, this implies that changes in the explanatory variables will have their greatest impact on rescheduling probability near the midpoint of the distribution. Equation 5.21 is equivalent to its regression form:

$$\ln\left(\frac{P}{1-P}\right) = \beta_0 + \beta_1 \eta_1 + \cdots + \beta_k \eta_k + \varepsilon$$

Equation 5.22

Equation 5.22 expresses the log odds (or logit) of rescheduling as a linear combination of known functions, η_k, and unknown parameters, β_k, and ε, which is a normally distributed random variable with zero mean.

When the variates are continuous, the maximum likelihood procedure is the preferred estimation method for Equation 5.22. This method does not require data repetitions and allows every individual observation within the sample (i.e. country-year) to have a distinct rescheduling probability associated with it. Under very general conditions, this technique produces estimates which are consistent, asymptotically efficient and asymptotically normal (McFadden, 1973). Moreover, because of these asymptotic properties, the testing of hypotheses can proceed in a manner similar to the linear regression framework under normality.

End-Chapter Notes

1 The theory presented in this chapter was inspired by the ideas of Lancaster's, 1966 and 1971, 'new' approach to consumer behaviour and also from Domencich and McFadden's, 1975 application of discrete choice models to transport demand analysis.

2 A rescheduling observation is defined as all official or private debt rescheduling agreements, arrears, repudiations, or distressed refinancings. The precise definitions of these four components have been presented in Chapter 3, Note 4.

3 Both matrices $\mathbf{C}$ and $\mathbf{B}$ are assumed to hold for all the debtor countries in the population with each coefficient being determined by the intrinsic properties of the goods, services and tactics themselves. The interested reader should see Lancaster, 1966 for more on this issue.

4 The utility function, U, is assumed to possess the property of additive separability so that $U(\mathbf{s},\mathbf{x},\mathbf{z}) = u(\mathbf{s},\mathbf{x}) - u(\mathbf{s},\mathbf{z})$. The interested reader should refer to McFadden, 1973 for more detail on this issue as it relates to discrete choice modelling.

5 The distribution of the error term has not yet been specified.

6 Alternatively, the linear probability function is obtained on the assumption that $(\varepsilon_{0j} - \varepsilon_{1j})$ is described by a uniform distribution. In this case, $P_{1jt}(\mathbf{\theta},\mathbf{z},\mathbf{r}) = ((V_1 - V_0)/\sigma)'\mathbf{\beta}$; which leads to $P_{1jt} = \beta_0 + \beta_1\eta_1 + \cdots + \beta_k\eta_k$. The uniform distribution implies a constant elasticity of rescheduling probability, β_k, over the entire interval of each explanatory variable, η_k. From an economic theoretical viewpoint, this property is not as appealing as the logistic function. However, unlike the logistic function, this cumulative density function allows the use of more complex econometric estimators. Hence, along with the logit model, the linear probability functional form will also be empirically tested in Chapter 6.

7 Non-compressible imports are considered to be a 'rigid' debtor-country policy variable since a forced reduction of their level would result in a decline in the economy's rate of growth, a reduction of its basic standard of living, and/or diminished creditworthiness. The exact proportion of non-compressible imports to total imports depends on country-specific factors which are determined by the debtor's long-

term structural constraints to creditworthiness. Pursuit of a rapid growth target, second-stage import substitution, or a binding absorptive capacity constraint for domestic capital goods would each introduce this element of rigidity into the borrower's import structure. See Avramovic *et al.*, 1964 for the initial exposition of this aspect of creditworthiness; refer to Grossman and Solberg, 1983 for its application to a cash-flow model of USSR creditworthiness.

8   While the ratio of non-compressible imports to total imports would be the theoretically preferred indicator, data limitations for the large sample preclude its use for empirical testing. Hence, $MGDP_{t-1}$ (rescheduling cost) is defined as the ratio of total expenditures on imported goods and services to gross domestic product. This indicator is lagged one year vis-à-vis the rescheduling observation. It is assumed that $MGDP_{t-1}$ is a predetermined attribute of the rescheduling choice mode. By measuring the 'price' of rescheduling, this indicator should have a negative correlation with rescheduling probability.

9   $COST_t$ (non-rescheduling cost) is defined as the difference between (1) the ratio of the sum of the scheduled amortization plus interest payments to total export receipts of goods and services, and (2) the ratio of the average private grant equivalent (that is, the commitment value of the loan less the discounted present value of its contractual debt service) to the amount committed. Thus, the cost or 'price' of non-rescheduling, $COST_t$, is comprised of a predetermined debtor country policy variable and an exogenously-determined prospective variable, respectively. This composite variable is specified contemporaneously with the rescheduling observation. The future loan cost of private debt only was used since it is more responsive than official debt terms to changes in market perceived creditworthiness. A rational borrowing strategy (that is, a downward-sloped demand curve for non-rescheduling or continued borrowing) would imply a positive relationship between this cost indicator and rescheduling probability.

10   A balance of payments disequilibrium comprises a structural, cyclical and stochastic component since the underlying determinant variables also exhibit these trends. While orthodox balance of payments theory is concerned with the comparative statics or dynamics of the adjustment mechanism, the origin of the imbalance or the type of disequilibrium is seldom addressed. By analysing the cause of the disequilibrium, however, the foreign-exchange budget constraints to per capita GDP growth and thus long-term creditworthiness are specified. Polak, 1948; Bernstein, 1958; and Villarreal, 1980 cite the importance of identifying the origins of an external disequilibrium, albeit for different purposes than creditworthiness assessment.

11   $ICOR_{t-5\text{ to }t-1}$ (structural budget constraint) is defined as the ratio of the share of gross fixed investment in GDP to the real growth rate of GDP. This indicator is computed as a five-year moving average which is then lagged one year vis-à-vis the rescheduling observation. It is assumed that the incremental capital-output ratio (or the inverse of the marginal efficiency of investment), ICOR, is a predetermined debtor country policy variable. Since a higher ICOR indicates a lower level of

investment efficiency, a positive correlation with rescheduling probability is postulated.

12 $PPP_{t-3 \text{ to } t-1}$ (adjustment budget constraint) is defined as the ratio of the debtor's consumer price index (1975 = 100) to industrial countries' consumer price index divided by the debtor's currency value vis-à-vis Special Drawing Rights (SDR). It is computed as a three-year moving average which is then lagged one year with respect to the rescheduling observation. The relative purchasing power parity index, PPP, is considered to be a predetermined debtor country trade adjustment policy variable. It is a measure of the debtor's global price competitiveness. A PPP index over 1.00 indicates overvaluation of the country's currency relative to the base year of 1975, while a value under 1.00 implies undervaluation. Besides distorting the allocation of domestic investment between tradable and non-tradable goods, an overvalued currency weakens export competitiveness and encourages imports expenditures and capital flight. Since these trends worsen the debtor's medium-term creditworthiness, the PPP index is a composite proxy for domestic price, income and monetary imbalances as they affect foreign exchange flows in the current and capital accounts. This indicator is postulated to be positively correlated with a country's rescheduling probability.

13 Dhonte, 1974, postulated an equilibrium condition comprising debt involvement (that is, stock level of debt and its flow requirement) and debt terms (that is, average debt service payments). Payment difficulties can occur when heavy debt involvement is combined with unfavourable borrowing terms or conditions.

14 $DODR_{t-1}$ (liquidity budget constraint) is defined as the ratio of total disbursed external debt to the sum of gold (national valuation) and foreign exchange holdings, including Special Drawing Rights. This indicator, DODR, is a predetermined debtor country liquidity variable which is lagged one year vis-à-vis the rescheduling observation. By comparing the stock magnitude of indebtedness to the current stock of international reserves, this indicator measures the debtor's past reliance on external net capital flows vis-à-vis its prior foreign exchange savings. This variable is also indicative of future debt service payments relative to the country's ability to finance these outflows from foreign exchange reserves. Nearly all cases of debt rescheduling have exhibited a high degree of debt involvement for which the debt to reserves ratio is considered to be the best indicator since it measures a stock against another stock. It is postulated to be positively correlated with the probability of rescheduling.

15 While the ratio of non-compressible to total imports is the theoretically preferred attribute value or price of the non-rescheduling choice mode, data limitations preclude its use in practice. Although imports to GDP is the indicator used for empirical work, non-compressible imports will continue to be used in the theoretical discussion as the attribute for the non-rescheduling choice mode.

16 The variates must satisfy regularity conditions so that the estimates converge to the true parameters as the sample size grows to infinity.

6.
Empirical Results of the Debt-Rescheduling Risk Model

6.1 Introduction

This chapter presents the empirical results of the rescheduling risk model developed in the previous two chapters. In section 6.2 certain univariate and multivariate test statistics are presented to examine the characteristics of the data base (sixty-seven developing countries over the period from 1971 to 1984).

The regression results of the linear probability model are presented in section 6.3. The model is specified using both a linear and quadratic Taylor approximation of the explanatory variables. The ordinary least squares technique is used to obtain the parameter estimates of this model. Chow tests, which check the stability of the estimated coefficients both across key country groups and over time, are shown in section 6.4. Certain *a priori* expectations concerning the changing determinants of sovereign creditworthiness over the sample period are tested. The economic implications of these tests are discussed.

This chapter also addresses certain statistical and data-related problems related to modelling sovereign debt rescheduling risk. In section 6.5 a fixed-effects specification is tested in order to extract more information from the panel data. To improve the efficiency of the coefficients, a 'modified' generalized least squares estimator is presented in section 6.6.

The logit probability model (a non-linear function) is presented in section 6.7. A maximum likelihood estimator is used to fit this new demand function to the panel data. The results of the logit model are contrasted with the results of the linear probability models in section 6.8. It concludes that the debtor countries, facing numerous tightened income constraints (due to internal and external shocks) and a falling relative 'price' of rescheduling, responded rationally by demanding the rescheduling choice mode.

6.2 Data-Base Characteristics

Sample Size
One of the fundamental problems encountered in modelling debt rescheduling risk is the small number of historical rescheduling observations. Most prior studies have pooled cross-sectional and time-series (panel) data to create a sufficiently large sample space. This technique is also employed in this study, implying that each observation corresponds to a particular country and year. For example, the Chilean rescheduling of 1971 is considered to be a separate observation from the Chilean rescheduling of 1972. The use of panel data, however, requires a fixed-effects specification to discern separate time-invariant cross-sectional effects and cross-sectional invariant time-series effects of the explanatory variables.

The independent variables tested in this model are constructed from current account and national account data compiled in the International Monetary Fund's *International Financial Statistics*. Indicators utilizing external debt and other financial data are obtained from the *World Debt Tables* of the International Bank for Reconstruction and Development (IBRD). Rescheduling observation points were compiled by the author from a variety of sources.[1] The sample size of this study is larger than that used in any published paper on econometric debt rescheduling. It incorporates 770 observations covering sixty-seven developing countries over the period from 1971 to 1984.[2] As is shown in Table 6.1, country representation is evenly balanced across geographic regions and income levels, including virtually all market-oriented developing countries with significant cross-border debt obligations.[3]

The sample countries listed in Table 6.1 are first grouped according to their oil dependence. The non-oil developing countries are further sub-classified according to their per capita income level (IBRD, 1983). Five of the thirteen net-oil exporters represent major oil producers during the entire sample period (for example, Indonesia, Iran, Iraq, Nigeria and Venezuela). The oil exporting group totals 155 observation points or approximately 20 per cent of the entire sample.

The remaining 80 per cent of the sample observations comprise the non-oil developing countries. This group is divided into high, middle and low income debtor countries, depending upon their level of per capita income in 1981 US dollars (IBRD, 1983). A country whose per capita income equals or exceeds $1,700 (in 1981 prices) is defined as a high income debtor. This group accounts for 17 per cent of the total sample. Most of these economies are newly industrialized countries (NICs), exhibiting rapid economic growth with a dynamic, diversified export sector which includes numerous

Table 6.1 Sample Observations for Sixty-Seven Developing Countries

Country	Observation	Country	Observation
I. *Net Oil Exporter*			
Bolivia	1971–1984	Mexico	1971–1984
Ecuador	1971–1983	Nigeria[1]	1971–1979,
Egypt	1971, 1973–1984		1982–1983
Indonesia[1]	1971–1984	Peru	1971–1984
Iran[1]	1971–1981	Trinidad and Tobago	1971–1980,
Iraq[1]	1971–1976		1982–1983
Malaysia	1971–1973	Tunisia	1971–1984
		Venezuela[1]	1971–1984
II. *Non-Oil Developing Countries*			
A. *High-Income Debtor*			
Argentina	1971–1983	Republic of Korea	1971–1984
Brazil	1971–1984	Portugal	1973–1983
Chile[2]	1971–1984	Spain	1971–1981
Costa Rica[2]	1971–1983	Uruguay[2]	1971–1984
Greece	1971–1984	Yugoslavia	1971–1980,
			1982–1984
B. *Middle Income Debtor*			
Barbados	1973–1982	Liberia	1976–1984
Botswana	1977–1983	Malta	1971–1984
Cameroon	1971–1974,	Mauritius	1971–1979, 1982
	1982–1984	Morocco	1971–1984
Colombia	1971–1984	Nicaragua	1971–1972,
Cyprus	1971–1984		1976–1984
Dominican	1971–1983	Panama	1971–1984
Republic		Papua New Guinea	1974–1983
El Salvador	1971–1983	Paraguay	1971–1984
Ghana	1971–1978, 1982	Philippines	1971–1974,
Guatemala	1971–1983		1982–1984
Guyana	1971–1984	Senegal	1971–1981
Honduras	1971–1984	Thailand	1971–1984
Jamaica	1971–1983	Turkey	1971–1981
Jordan	1971–1974,	Yemen Arab	
	1982–1984	Republic	1975–1983
Kenya	1971–1984	Zambia	1971–1984
III. *Low Income Debtor*			
Burma	1971–1984	Sierra Leone	1971–1983
Ethiopia	1971–1984	Sri Lanka	1971–1984
Haiti	1972–1981	Sudan	1971–1973
India	1971–1980,	Tanzania	1971–1981
	1982–1983	Togo	1971–1981
Madagascar	1971–1981	Uganda	1971–1981
Malawi	1971–1983	Upper Volta	1971
Mauritania	1971	Zaire	1971–1981
Pakistan	1971–1984		

Notes: [1] Major oil exporter.
[2] Not a major exporter of manufactured goods.

manufactured products. Despite possessing high per capita income, Chile, Costa Rica and Uruguay represent exceptions within this group, since they exhibit an extreme concentration of primary products in exports.

The middle income non-oil developing countries have a per capita income level between US $400 and US $1,700. They account for the largest sub-group in the sample, representing 42 per cent of the total observations. Finally, all countries with per capita income below US $400 were classified as low income debtors. This group contributes 21 per cent of the sample observations.

The number of rescheduling observations (114) is small compared with the 656 cases of non-rescheduling, representing only 15 per cent of the total sample points. However, the incidence of rescheduling points within the prior country groupings, is broadly consistent with the overall distribution of the sample. A plurality of rescheduling observations (33 per cent) is found in the largest debtor group (that is, middle income). The low income debtors contribute the second largest number of rescheduling points (25 per cent). The net-oil exporters and the high income debtors supply the smallest proportion of rescheduling points, equalling 23 per cent and 19 per cent, respectively. The rescheduling observations comprise forty different countries and are distributed over the entire time period (see Table 6.2).

Since both the historical classification efficiency and the predictive ability of the debt model are tested, the sample is divided into a base-year period, 1971–1981, and out-of-sample period, 1982–1984. The within-sample period (used to estimate the population parameters), includes sixty-nine rescheduling points, representing 61 per cent of the total reschedulings and twenty-seven different debtors (68 per cent of the rescheduling countries). The observations within the hold-out period (used to measure the prospective efficiency of the model), comprise 45 rescheduling points, covering 28 countries of which 12 did not reschedule in the prior period.

Univariate and Multivariate Sample Statistics
The classification efficiency of the model's rescheduling probabilities is determined by the statistical characteristics of the explanatory variables. The model's error rates are higher, the closer the 'score' (that is, the mean relative to the standard deviation) of the variates for the rescheduling versus the non-rescheduling group. Model efficiency improves when the overlap between the distributions of the rescheduling and non-rescheduling sub-groups narrows.

The sample data reveal that for the non-rescheduling group, the average attribute value or price of the rescheduling choice mode – the ratio of merchandise imports to GDP (MGDP) – is larger than

Table 6.2   Sovereign Rescheduling Sample Observations,
1971–1984

I.   Original Sample Observations, 1971–1981

Year	Countries
1971	Chile, Egypt, India, Pakistan, Yugoslavia
1972	Chile, Ghana, India, Pakistan, Peru, Turkey
1973	Chile, Egypt, India, Pakistan
1974	Chile, Ghana, India, Indonesia, Pakistan
1975	Chile, India, Uruguay, Zaire
1976	Argentina, India, Mexico, Peru, Zaire
1977	Ecuador, Egypt, India, Sierra Leone, Turkey, Zaire
1978	India, Jamaica, Peru, Turkey
1979	Guyana, Iran, Jamaica, Togo, Turkey, Zaire
1980	Bolivia, Iran, Jamaica, Liberia, Nicaragua, Peru, Sierra Leone, Togo, Turkey, Yugoslavia, Zaire
1981	Bolivia, Costa Rica, Haiti, Iran, Jamaica, Liberia, Madagascar, Nicaragua, Pakistan, Senegal, Togo, Uganda, Zaire

II.   'Hold-Out' Sample Observations, 1982–1984

1982	Guyana, Honduras, Liberia, Malawi, Mexico, Nicaragua
1983	Argentina, Bolivia, Brazil, Chile, Costa Rica, Dominican Republic, Ecuador, Guyana, Jamaica, Liberia, Malawi, Mexico, Morocco, Nicaragua, Nigeria, Panama, Peru, Uruguay, Venezuela, Yugloslavia, Zambia
1984	Bolivia, Brazil, Chile, Colombia, Guyana, Honduras, Liberia, Mexico, Morocco, Nicaragua, Panama, Peru, Philippines, Tunisia, Uruguay, Venezuela, Yugoslavia, Zambia

that of the rescheduling group (see Table 6.3). This supports the *a priori* expectation developed in Chapter 5. However, there is considerable overlap between these two groups, given the large value of the respective standard deviations relative to the differential between the means.[4]

The sample value of the debt service cost variable for the two sub groups also supports the *a priori* notion that the non-rescheduling group faced a lower price or cost of sustainable borrowing. This is true for every quartile of the sample. Similar to the rescheduling choice mode attribute, however, there is considerable overlap of the two sample distributions.

Assume the relative price of rescheduling versus non-rescheduling is computed as the quotient of the two choice-mode means. Since the relative price of rescheduling for the rescheduling group (0.8) was only one-fifth of that for the non-rescheduling group (3.7), it is not surprising that the former group opted for the

Table 6.3 Sample Characteristics of Non-Rescheduling and Rescheduling Groups, 1971–1984

	Non-Rescheduling Group					Rescheduling Group				
	Choice modes		Budget constraints liquidity adjustment solvency			Choice modes		Budget constraints liquidity adjustment solvency		
	Rescheduling cost	Non-rescheduling cost				Rescheduling cost	Non-rescheduling cost			
Statistic	MGDP	Debt-Service Cost	DODR	PPP^y	ICOR	MGDP	Debt-Service Cost	DODR	PPP^y	ICOR
Mean	34.4	9.3	7.7	1.05	7.4	30.6	40.7	25.2	1.15	10.0
Standard deviation	19.2	17.4	22.3	0.53	17.9	19.8	247.0	45.0	0.59	16.8
Coefficient of variation (relative dispersion)	55.8	188.4	289.9	50.64	244.0	64.7	607.2	178.5	51.56	168.9
First quartile	20.6	1.0	1.4	0.91	2.4	15.2	6.8	5.7	0.88	2.5
Second quartile	30.3	5.5	3.4	0.98	3.7	25.6	16.8	10.3	0.99	5.1
Third quartile	43.1	16.3	6.7	1.07	6.4	42.6	33.1	19.9	1.14	9.8
Number of observations	807	828	851	822	725	131	129	141	130	129

rescheduling choice mode. Not only was the relative price of rescheduling cheaper for this group, but the three budget constraints were also tighter.

The liquidity constraint is binding when heavy debt involvement and costly debt terms combine to create large liability flows which exceed short-term foreign-exchange sources (that is, international reserves and loan disbursements). Since the mean level of indebtedness relative to international reserves for the rescheduling group was over three times higher than for the non-rescheduling group, most rescheduling cases involved a tightened liquidity constraint.

The adjustment and structural constraints were also tighter for the rescheduling group, as evidenced by larger mean values (see Table 6.3). Combined with the tighter liquidity constraint, medium-term and long-term policy manoeuverability was more restricted than for the non-rescheduling group. In particular, the mean value of the relative purchasing power parity index (PPP) for the rescheduling group shows that average real exchange rates were 15 per cent overvalued relative to the base period. In contrast, average real exchange rates were only 5 per cent overvalued for the non-rescheduling group.

Similarly, the mean value of the incremental capital-output ratio (ICOR) for the rescheduling group was over 35 per cent higher than for the non-rescheduling group. A higher ICOR (that is, a lower marginal efficiency of investment) implies that the rescheduling group was less able than the non-rescheduling group to translate new borrowings into economic growth and structural change.

Tests for normality were conducted prior to the testing for the independence of sample means between the rescheduling and non-rescheduling groups (see Table 6.4). According to the Kolmogorov-Smirnov D-Statistic tested at the 1 per cent level, only the debt-service cost variable for the non-rescheduling group is normally distributed. Plots of all the variables, classified by rescheduling and non-rescheduling groups, also confirm that virtually all the variates are not normally distributed.[5]

To ascertain the independence of rescheduling and non-rescheduling groups means for each of the five continuous explanatory variables, two non-parametric univariate tests (the Wilcoxon T-test and the Kruskal-Wallis H-test) were conducted besides the usual Z-test, because of the suspected non-normality of the sample. At least two of the three testing procedures confirm that all but one of the explanatory variables (ICOR) reveal significant differences of group means at the 5 per cent level. The structural constraint (ICOR) was able to reject the null hypothesis in only one of the three tests, suggesting the possible equality of rescheduling

Table 6.4 Univariate and Multivariate Test Statistics of Sample Characteristics

Variable	Kolmogorov-Smirnov D-Statistic[1] Reject H_0 $Y = 0$	Reject H_0 $Y = 1$	Normal Z-Statistic[2] Statistic	Reject H_0	Wilcoxon T-Statistic[3] Statistic	Reject H_0	Kruskal–Wallis H-Statistic[3] Statistic	Reject H_0	Hotelling–Lawley T^0 Statistic[4] Reject H_0	Roy's Root[4] Reject H_0	Box's Approximate Chi-squared[5] Reject H_0
COST	No	Yes	−5.34	Yes	31,535	Yes	28.73	Yes	Yes	Yes	Yes
MGDP	Yes	Yes	4.32	Yes	15,637	No	20.42	Yes	Yes	Yes	Yes
DODR	Yes	Yes	−3.33	Yes	40,806	Yes	75.26	Yes	Yes	Yes	Yes
PPP	Yes	Yes	−2.38	Yes	30,324	Yes	1.64	No	Yes	Yes	Yes
ICOR	Yes	Yes	−0.40	No	17,811	Yes	0.00	No	Yes	Yes	Yes

Notes:
1 An empirical density function test for the normality of these subgroups; H_0: sample distributed normally. Tested at the 1% level.
2 The normal Z-test for the independence of group means; H_0: $X_0 = X_1$, tested at the 5% level.
3 A non-parametric test for the independence of group means; H_0: $X_0 = X_1$, tested at the 5% level.
4 A multivariate test for the independence of group means; H_0: $X_{i0} = X_{i1}$, $i = 1, \ldots, 5$; tested at the 1% level.
5 A multivariate test for the equality of the dispersion matrices; H_0: $Z_0 = Z_1$, tested at the 1% level.

and non-rescheduling group means. Two additional tests were conducted to check for the difference between multivariate group means. The Hotelling-Lawley Trace and Roy's Greatest Characteristic Root both showed highly significant group differences at the 1 per cent level for all five variates (see Table 6.4).

A final test was conducted for the equality of the dispersion matrices. As is shown in Table 6.4, Box's approximate $F_{30.6}$ statistic of 152.7 rejects the null hypothesis, implying that the dispersion or variance-covariance matrices for the rescheduling and non-rescheduling groups are unequal.[6] This implies that a quadratic rather than a linear function may be appropriate for the rescheduling demand model. Therefore, empirical testing will include both the non-linear logistic function and a second-order approximation of the Taylor expansion in the linear probability model.

The univariate and multivariate statistics shown in Tables 6.3 and 6.4 support the *a priori* theoretical postulates of debt service capacity presented in Chapter 5. The one-year liquidity, three-year adjustment, and five-year structural budget constraints for the rescheduling group were all 'tighter' than for the non-rescheduling group.[7]

The attribute value or price of sustained borrowing or non-rescheduling (that is, debt-service cost) was greater for the rescheduling group, while the price of rescheduling (MGDP) was higher for the non-rescheduling group. Thus, the 'relative price' of rescheduling versus sustained borrowing for the rescheduling group was considerably lower than that faced by the non-rescheduling group. Therefore, with limited policy manoeuverability (as shown by the tightened budget constraints), and facing a lower relative price for the rescheduling choice mode, the illiquid and perhaps insolvent debtor acted rationally by maximizing perceived utility and choosing the consumption activity vector which included the least costly rescheduling choice-mode option.

6.3   Linear Probability Model

The Linear Model

The results of the linear probability model, using the ordinary least squares estimator, generally support the relationship postulated between the explanatory variables and rescheduling probability. The classification efficiency of this model, both within- and out-of-sample, was similar to the range of efficiency rates found in other published studies.

In Model 1, all the estimated parameters have the expected sign (see Table 6.5). With the exception of the long-term structural constraint variable, which does not meet the 10 per cent test, all the estimated parameters are highly significant. The coefficient for rescheduling cost is significant at the 5 per cent level, while all the remaining variables are significant at the 1 per cent level, or better.[8] The F-statistic is highly significant at the 1 per cent level, thus rejecting the null hypothesis that all the model's coefficients are equal to zero.

The coefficient for debt-service cost measures the current and prospective price which the debtor pays for continued borrowing or non-rescheduling. As expected, it indicates that a borrower's rescheduling probability rises as the cost of servicing foreign debt increases.

The negative coefficient for rescheduling cost also supports the *a priori* contention that, as the price of rescheduling rises (that is, as measured by the potential magnitude of foregone imports, MGDP), the probability of rescheduling declines. The relative size of these two 'price' elasticities indicates that a 1 per cent increase in the cost of rescheduling lowers the probability of rescheduling by twice as much as a 1 per cent increase in the debt service costs raises the rescheduling probability.

The coefficient for the rescheduling state variable (which measures the debtor's past cumulative experience with rescheduling) confirms that this variable has a strong positive effect on prospective rescheduling behaviour. Hence, once a country has had to reschedule its debt, it is likely that this past borrowing strategy will be repeated. This indicator incorporates unspecified effects which positively impact the probability of debt rescheduling (for example, inadequate debt relief from prior reschedulings or a credit supply constraint).

The coefficients for each of the structural, adjustment and liquidity budget-constraint characteristics are all positive. These positive relationships show that, as each of the three constraints is tightened (that is, lower investment efficiency, declining international price competitiveness, and a higher net stock of foreign exchange liabilities, respectively), the probability of rescheduling increases. The relative size of the coefficients indicates that the debtor's international price competitiveness possesses the greatest marginal impact on rescheduling probability, while the stock of foreign liabilities relative to external assets and the marginal efficiency of investment have a lesser effect.

For this data, the diagnostics suggest that multicollinearity amongst the explanatory variables is not a major problem. Computed from the full sample period (that is, 1971–1984), the correlation matrix for the explanatory variables is shown in the top

Table 6.5 Ordinary Least Squares Linear Probability Model, 1971–1981

Rescheduling Demand Indicators	Model 1 (First-order approximation)		Model 2 (Second-order approximation)	
	Coefficient	T-statistic	Coefficient	T-statistic
A. Rescheduling-mode attributes				
Debt-service cost	0.0005	3.86	−0.0002	−0.98
Rescheduling cost	−0.001	−1.70	−0.008	−3.94
[Rescheduling cost]^2	n.a.	n.a.	0.0001	3.66
Rescheduling state	0.082	7.43	0.077	7.04
B. Budget-constraint characteristics				
Long-term structural	0.001	1.02	0.005	2.73
[Long-term structural]^2	n.a.	n.a.	−0.00005	−2.26
Medium-term adjustment	0.114	3.47	0.092	2.82
Short-term liquidity	0.010	6.74	0.016	6.17
[Short-term liquidity]^2	n.a.	n.a.	−0.0001	−2.59
Intercept	−0.091	−2.00	−0.003	−0.36
Adjusted R^2	.21		.23	
F-statistic	26.69		21.05	
Durbin–Watson statistic	1.468		1.531	
Maximum condition index	9.6		18.7	

half of Table 6.6. Pairwise correlations between each of the explanatory variables are insignificant, with the possible exception of the positive correlation (.38) between the debt service cost variable (COST) and the liquidity constraint variable (DODR). Although this simple diagnostic will detect serious collinearity between any two variables, more complex interrelationships must be detected using matrix decompositions. Thus, to support the conclusion of minimal multicollinearity, the matrix decomposition test recommended by Belsley, Kuh and Welsch (1980) is conducted. As shown in the bottom half of Table 6.6, the variance proportions matrix contains very low values for the condition index. This supports the conclusion drawn above.[9]

A one-sided diagnostic test for autocorrelated errors was also conducted using the Durbin-Watson d-statistic shown in Table 6.5. This test for positive first-order autocorrelation rejects the null hypothesis at the 5 per cent level.[10] Therefore, it is plausible to expect first-order autocorrelation in this data base. In this case, the residual error estimate is inflated and the t-tests are less able to show significant coefficients. Since the normal remedies for this problem (for example, Cochrane-Orcutt, Hildreth-Lu procedures, etc.) cannot be applied to a binary-valued dependent-variable model, this issue is not pursued further.

Two measures of the model's goodness of fit are presented. The first is the usual adjusted coefficient of determination or R^2. For Model 1, the portion of the total variance explained by the model (after being adjusted for degrees of freedom) is 21 per cent. In gauging the model's efficacy, it must be remembered that the R^2 for a binary-valued dependent-variable model is not likely to range between the typical limits of 0 and 1. In fact, it may have an upper bound of only 0.33, assuming that the distribution of the score is uniform over the unit interval.[11] With this assumption, nearly two-thirds of the total sample variance is explained by Model 1.

A preferred method for assessing the model's goodness of fit is to measure the classification efficiency of the predicted dependent variable against both actual historical observations and hold-out data of the dependent variable. Once a critical (or cut-off) value is determined, each predicted rescheduling probability can be classified as either a rescheduling ($Y = 1$) or non-rescheduling ($Y = 0$) occurrence.[12] When compared to actual rescheduling behaviour, the classification efficiency can be determined and used as a goodness of fit measure.

A Type I error occurs when a country-year classified as a non-rescheduling observation actually corresponds to a rescheduling case (that is, a false non-rescheduling prediction). Conversely, a Type II error is a non-rescheduling country-year incorrectly

Table 6.6 Correlation Matrix and Multicollinearity Diagnostics for Full Sample, 1971–1984.

A Correlation matrix

	INTERCEPT	STATE	DODR	PPP	ICOR	MGDP	COST
INTERCEPT	1						
STATE	-.24	1					
DODR	-.03	-.20	1				
PPP	-.81	.04	-.04	1			
ICOR	-.08	-.04	.03	.01	1		
MGDP	-.58	.12	-.13	.16	-.09	1	
COST	-.05	.05	.38	.04	-.002	-.08	1

B Variance proportions for Model 1, 1971–1984

Number	Eigen-value	Condition index	Portion INTERCEPT	Portion STATE	Portion DODR	Portion PPP	Portion ICOR	Portion MGDP	Portion COST
1	3.703	1.00	0.005	0.022	0.020	0.007	0.015	0.014	0.004
2	1.139	1.80	.001	0.001	0.111	0.002	0.055	0.005	0.482
3	0.801	2.15	.001	0.053	0.038	0.003	0.851	0.001	0.086
4	0.616	2.45	0.005	0.719	0.017	0.011	0.057	0.049	0.024
5	0.468	2.81	0.003	0.116	0.832	0.006	0.014	0.000	0.393
6	0.226	4.05	0.011	0.051	0.017	0.182	0.005	0.650	0.008
7	0.047	8.88	0.974	0.039	0.001	0.789	0.002	0.281	0.003

categorized as a rescheduling point. The respective error rates are computed as the ratio of each of these error frequencies to the maximum number of Type I and Type II errors which are possible. For classification of the within-sample period (1971–81), these maximum values are 70 and 535, respectively; while the respective data for the hold-out period (1982–84) are 44 and 121.

The classification error rates for Model 1 are reported in Table 6.7. With a critical value of 19 per cent, only 8 observations or 12 per cent of the 70 rescheduling cases were misclassified in the historical sample. The false rescheduling classifications of the Type II error rate equalled 45 per cent. The out-of-sample or predictive efficiency of the model is slightly lower. Thirteen rescheduling observations, or 29 per cent, were misclassified, while 42 non-rescheduling observations, or 35 per cent, were incorrect. Ostensibly, these historical classification rates do not represent any improvement over prior studies. However, Heller (1980) has observed that the estimated parameters can be extremely sensitive to sample size and composition. Thus, it is likely that the seemingly efficient results of prior studies are due, in part, to their relatively small sample sizes. Therefore, the results of this study compare favourably with prior studies when account is taken for its larger and more diverse data set.

A Second-Order Taylor Approximation
Model 2 is derived from those variables in Model 1 plus the squared and interaction terms as derived from a second-order approximation of the Taylor series expansion. The regression results for this specification are shown in Table 6.5 and its classification efficiency is presented in Table 6.7.

Using a one-sided test, only three of the additional terms proved to have coefficients which were significant at the 2.5 per cent level or better. The squared rescheduling cost variable ($MGDP^2$), the long-term structural constraint (ICOR), and the short-term liquidity constraint (DODR).

The goodness of fit for Model 2 has improved only moderately compared to that of Model 1. Whether measured by the adjusted R^2 statistic or by the model's historical or prospective classification efficiency, the second-order Taylor specification provides a better fit of the data than does the first-order approximation. As with Model 1, however, the out-of-sample error rates deteriorate vis-à-vis those generated within the sample. Each of the other statistics (the maximum condition index, the Durbin-Watson d-statistic and the F statistic) result in conclusions which are identical to those obtained from Model 1.

On balance, the first-order terms in Model 2 are more significant

Table 6.7 Historical Classification and Predictive Efficiency of Rescheduling Demand Models (percentage)

Specification	Within sample (1971–1981)			Out of sample (1982–1984)		
	Cut-off probability[e]	Type I error rate[f]	Type II error rate[g]	Cut-off probability[e]	Type I error rate[f]	Type II error rate[g]
Model 1[a]	19	12	45	17	29	35
Model 2[a]	20	12	40	11	30	27
Model 3[b]	22	17	27	n.a.	n.a.	n.a.
Model 4[c]	32	38	16	47	22	34
Model 5[c]	50	24	37	57	28	40
Model 6[d]	10	26	28	11	41	13
Model 7[d]	11	21	30	7	32	33

Notes:
[a] See Table 6.5.
[b] See Table 6.8.
[c] See Table 6.9.
[d] See Table 6.10.
[e] The critical value is chosen so as to minimize the cumulative sum of the Type I and Type II error rates.
[f] False non-rescheduling prediction.
[g] False rescheduling prediction.

than those in Model 1. The debt service cost variable is the only exception. Its sign has changed and can no longer pass the significance test, even at the 10 per cent level. The significance of the first-order terms for rescheduling cost and the long-term structural constraint has improved, showing significance at the 1 per cent level or better. All the other coefficients, remaining highly significant, are virtually unchanged from those in Model 1.

Each of the quadratic terms have signs which are opposite to their respective linear terms, supporting the concept of diminishing marginal returns. A percentage increase in an already tight budget constraint will increase rescheduling probability by a smaller amount than an equal percentage increase in its value when the budget constraint is less tight.

The sign of the quadratic term for rescheduling cost implies that the 'price' elasticity of rescheduling demand is fairly elastic for a debtor with a small ratio of imports to GDP. Conversely, it is more inelastic for a debtor with a large ratio of imports to GDP. Assuming diminishing marginal utility from the consumption of imported merchandise, the marginal disutility from forced import reduction at very high import levels will be less than the marginal disutility of credit-constrained import reduction at lower import-to-GDP levels. This may be true for several reasons.

A country with a high level of imports to GDP is likely to be importing a higher proportion of compressible imports. This component would comprise not only consumer goods but also investment and intermediate goods which are funding projects which may not meet all of the solvency criteria; hence they are compressible. For example, a high level of imports may be due to an aggressive investment programme which has also resulted in domestic bottlenecks and caused the ICOR to rise. In this case, the rates of return on investment programmes at the margin are unlikely to exceed the external cost of funds. Thus, the cost to this debtor of eliminating this portion of imports would be much smaller than the cost borne by a country with a 'leaner' composition of imports.

Another reason for the sign of the second-order coefficient may be related to the openness of the economy. Countries with a higher level of imports to GDP are usually pursuing a development strategy based on export promotion rather than import substitution. Balassa (1980) has argued that the adjustment capability of export-promoting countries is more flexible (and hence, presumably less costly) than import-substituting countries. If this is true, then the cost associated with a similar percentage reduction of imports for a large importer would be less than that for a smaller importer.

The sign of the quadratic term for the long-term structural constraint implies that a rising incremental capital-output ratio will have a diminishing deleterious effect on rescheduling probability.

Similarly, the sign of the quadratic term for the short-term liquidity constraint indicates that rising net external liabilities will increase the debtor's rescheduling probability at a diminishing marginal rate. This is certainly plausible. Once a country's debt level becomes extremely high, relative power of financial negotiation concerning debt rescheduling shifts in favour of the debtor. Hence, even if the debtor is not perceived to be creditworthy, it can extract additional money from the external creditors by threatening default (debt repudiation). By receiving this new money (in effect, by extortion), the debtor postpones a debt rescheduling and lowers its rescheduling probability. A country with a smaller debt level which is perceived not to be creditworthy, cannot extract new money as easily since the potential impact of repudiation on the creditor's balance sheet is minimal. Hence, the marginal impact on rescheduling probability of an increase in the net liabilities for a small debtor would be higher due to its impaired ability to roll over its maturities.

6.4   Stability of Estimated Coefficients

Since panel data were used, it was necessary to test for the stability of the coefficients both over time and across particular country types. Hence, Chow (1960) tests were conducted to check the model's structural homogeneity.

The first set of Chow tests measure the stability of the coefficients in Model 1 over three distinct time periods: 1971–1974, 1975–1979 and 1980–1984. This division is based on the assumption that the oil-price shock of 1973–1974 and again in 1979–1980 significantly changed the character of the global commodity and financial markets. These changes, in turn, are anticipated to have altered the determinants of sovereign rescheduling probability.

The unrestricted residual sum of squares is obtained by adding the residual sum of squares for each pair of equations. Next, the two combinations of contiguous groupings for the three time periods are estimated with the same econometric specification, although with seven linear restrictions (that is, $a(1) = a(2)$, $B_1(1) = B_1(2)$, . . . , $B_6(1) = B_6(2)$). Thus, the restricted residual sum of squares is obtained which, combined with the prior information, allows two separate F tests on the stability of the rescheduling demand coefficients between each of the two contiguous time periods.

The results of these two F tests were insignificant at the 5 per cent level. Hence, the null hypotheses are not rejected. That is, the coefficients from the two pairs of contiguous time periods are not necessarily different. A final Chow test for the periods 1971–1974 and 1980–1984 was conducted and found to be significant at the 5 per cent level. As a result of this test (which implies that structural change did occur), Model 2 is altered to include a cross-section invariant, time-series fixed-effects specification. However, before this new model is presented, the results of the Chow tests across several country groupings will be discussed.

Analogous tests were conducted to measure the stability of coefficients across the four country types (net-oil exporters, high income, middle income, and low income non-oil developing countries). Three separate Chow tests were conducted across adjacent groupings (low income and middle income debtors; middle income and high income debtors; and high income and net-oil exporting debtors) over the full time period, 1971–84. Only the first test was significant at the 1 per cent level, thus implying substantive group differences between the low and middle income non-oil developing country debtors. The other two tests, between the middle income and high income debtors and between the high income debtors and the net-oil exporters, were insignificant at the 1 per cent level. Thus, the null hypothesis asserting common rescheduling demand coefficients over the 1970s and early 1980s for these final three groups cannot be rejected.

These results are intuitively plausible. All the developing countries which borrowed heavily from the private capital markets during the 1970s are included either in the net-oil exporting, the high income or middle income debtor groups. The perceived creditworthiness of these groups, in contrast to the low income countries, allowed them greater access to commercial bank credit which commonly affected their rescheduling probabilities.

With the exception of Zaire, Pakistan and the Sudan, the low income countries were not significant recipients of private commercial bank loans during the 1970s. A combination of low income levels and a paucity of energy resources reduced their perceived creditworthiness, limited their commercial borrowing (from the supply side) and thus significantly altered their determinants of rescheduling probability vis-à-vis the higher income groups. Hence, the low income group primarily relied on bilateral or multilateral loans and grants-in-aid which incorporated longer average maturities and lower interest rates.

The statistically significant differences across certain country groups suggest that a fixed effects specification is appropriate for the pooled data. Model 3 incorporates this fixed effects specification by adding cross-section and time-series dummy variables to Model 2. These results are presented in Table 6.8.

Table 6.8 Fixed Effects Linear Probability Model, 1971–1984

	Model 3	
Rescheduling demand indicators	Coefficient	T-statistic

A. *Rescheduling mode attributes*

	Coefficient	T-statistic
Debt service cost	0.0003	1.99
Rescheduling cost	−0.004	−1.06
[Rescheduling cost]^2	0.00003	0.91
Rescheduling state	0.0236	1.56

B. *Budget constraint characteristics*

	Coefficient	T-statistic
Long-term structural	0.0007	0.63
[Long-term structural]^2	−0.000005	−0.94
Medium-term adjustment	0.095	2.71
Short-term liquidity	0.015	5.69
[Short-term liquidity]^2	−0.00008	−2.73

C. *Year dummy variables*

Year	Coefficient	Year	Coefficient
1971	0.209	1978	−.092
1972	−0.131	1979	−.119
1973	−0.097	1980	−.080
1974	−0.108	1981	.016
1975	−0.095	1982	−.026
1976	−0.118	1983	−.114
1977	−0.110	1984	.166

D. *Country dummy variables*

	Coefficient		Coefficient
Argentina	0.006	Iran	0.194
Barbados	0.083	Iraq	0.079
Bolivia	0.115	Jamaica	0.344
Botswana	0.068	Jordan	0.152
Brazil	0.001	Kenya	0.083
Burma	0.012	Korea (South)	−0.036
Cameroon	−0.112	Liberia	0.244
Chile	0.182	Madagascar	0.053
Colombia	0.031	Malawi	0.110
Costa Rica	0.203	Malaysia	−0.057
Cyprus	0.115	Malta	0.077
Dominican Republic	−0.008	Mauritania	−0.055
Ecuador	0.156	Mauritius	0.070
Egypt	0.219	Mexico	0.015
El Salvador	0.036	Morocco	0.019
Ethiopia	−0.063	Nicaragua	0.323
Ghana	0.189	Nigeria	0.178
Greece	−0.031	Pakistan	0.315
Guatamala	−0.012	Panama	−0.055
Guyana	0.066	Papua New Guinea	0.094
Haiti	0.123	Paraguay	−0.007
Honduras	0.069	Peru	0.416
India	0.811	Philippines	0.118
Indonesia	0.046	Portugal	0.084

	Coefficient		*Coefficient*
Senegal	−0.090	Turkey	0.508
Sierra Leone	0.210	Uganda	−0.063
Spain	0.108	Upper Volta	0.092
Sri Lanka	−0.016	Uruguay	0.169
Sudan	−0.049	Venezuela	0.167
Tanzania	−0.088	Yemen Arab Republic	0.165
Thailand	0.030	Yugoslavia	0.205
Togo	0.260	Zaire	0.461
Trinidad and Tobago	0.101	Zambia	—
Tunisia	0.008		

Adjusted R^2 = .40   F-statistic = 5.68   Durban-Watson statistic = 1.75

6.5 Fixed Effects

The coefficients in Model 3 are estimated using a least squares estimator. The coefficients for the nine explanatory variables from Model 2 are considered to be constant over time and countries. The time coefficients are assumed to be country invariant and the country coefficients are time invariant.

In comparison to Model 2, the nine original coefficients have not changed dramatically, although some of the original explanatory variables have lost some of their significance. Their signs are unchanged vis-à-vis Model 2, with the exception of the debt service cost variable. The sign of this parameter estimate in Model 3 probably represents the correct sign, since the coefficient was not significant in Model 2. Moreover, the sign of the coefficient for debt service cost in Model 3 is identical to that in Model 1 which, in turn, supports the *a priori* expectation for this rescheduling mode attribute. The coefficients for debt service cost, the adjustment, liquidity and quadratic liquidity budget constraint variables are all significant at the 2.5 per cent level, or better. The rescheduling state coefficient is significant at approximately the 6 per cent level, while those for the rescheduling cost, the structural budget constraint variable and their respective quadratic terms do not pass the 10 per cent test.

The coefficients for the country-invariant, time-dummy variables measure the yearly impact of global economic and financial conditions on average sovereign rescheduling probability. While the changes in these annual coefficients are broadly consistent with the timing of various shocks to the global financial system, these results must be interpreted gingerly since they average both oil-importing and oil-exporting country effects.

The relative magnitudes of the average yearly global rescheduling probabilities indicate the adverse impact of the oil-price shocks in 1974 and 1979, showing that the latter disturbance was more severe. The improvement in 1975 highlights the beneficial impact of the commodity price boom on the terms of trade for the developing countries. The declining average rescheduling probability in 1977 and 1978 may reflect the inflationary erosion of the real debt service payments and declining real oil prices during those years.

Systematic or average global creditworthiness actually improved in 1980 and 1981. Perhaps this was due to the ability of the debtors to postpone adjustment to the second oil shock owing to the dramatic increase in the net financial transfer which occurred in 1980 and 1981. Finally, in 1982 and 1983, new capital inflow was severely limited and the real cost of debt service reached nearly four times its level of 1980, due to the intensification of external shocks. The accelerating financial roll-over process of 1980 and 1981, which had postponed the day of reckoning, had broken down. The impact of the cumulative shocks hitting full force markedly worsened the systematic rescheduling probabilities in 1982 and 1983. The improvement in 1984 may be indicative of the recovery of OECD growth which boosted the export volume of developing countries, and coupled with the oil price drop, significantly improved their terms of trade.

The coefficients of the time-invariant country-dummy variables measure the average country-specific or non-systematic rescheduling probability. For this sample period, it appears that India, Jamaica, Nicaragua, Pakistan, Peru, Togo, Turkey and Zaire represent debtors with a relatively high 'inherent' rescheduling probability. On the other hand, Cameroon, Dominican Republic, Ethiopia, Greece, Guatemala, South Korea, Malaysia, Mauritania, Panama, Paraguay, Senegal, Sri Lanka, Sudan, Tanzania and Uganda possess particularly low country-specific rescheduling probabilities. Among the first group of eight countries it would appear that all are correctly classified, owing to the fact that they all rescheduled more than once during the sample period.

Of the fifteen countries which possess a low inherent rescheduling probability, only five (Dominican Republic, Panama, Senegal, Sudan and Uganda) would seem to be misclassified, since each of these rescheduled at least once since 1970. In the case of Sudan the misclassification results from there being only three complete observation points (between 1971 and 1973), while all of its rescheduling activity occurred much later. For the other four countries it is possible that key factors not specified in the model (for example, political instability, weak capacity to save, etc.) might explain the misclassification.

T values for the dummy variables are not listed in Table 9.8 since they are extremely sensitive to changes in the model's parameters. A joint test assessing the equality of the dummy variable coefficients is preferred to examining individual t statistics (Judge, Hill, Griffiths, Lutkepohl, and Lee, 1982). An F test of the null hypothesis that all the dummy variable coefficients were identical was significant at the 1 per cent level. Thus, the null hypothesis is rejected, implying that both time and country-specific effects are important for rescheduling risk modelling.

This conclusion is also supported by the generic test statistics and goodness-of-fit checks. The F statistic rejects the null hypothesis at the 1 per cent level, implying that all the model's coefficients are significantly different from zero. Both goodness-of-fit measures have improved dramatically compared to Models 1 or 2. The adjusted R^2 of .40 (which corrects for degrees of freedom) has almost doubled. As shown in Table 6.7 on p. 112, the historical classification error rates also have improved.

6.6   Weighted Least Squares

The ordinary least squares estimator is inefficient for the linear probability model. Hence, to obtain an efficient estimator, Goldberger (1964) recommends the use of a 'modified' generalized least squares (or weighted least squares) estimator. To address this problem, Table 6.9 presents the results of this new, efficient estimator. First, consistent estimates of the rescheduling probabilities are obtained using ordinary least squares. Next, every observation is weighted by the square root of the estimated error variance. Finally, ordinary least squares is performed on these transformed variables. The new estimates are not necessarily more efficient than ordinary least squares, since estimated probabilities are used in this two-stage estimation procedure. However, given the large data base these modified estimates should be unbiased, consistent and asymptotically efficient.

As can be seen in Table 6.9, the weighted least squares estimates for Model 4 all have the correct sign. The relative size of these coefficients are very similar to the ordinary least squares estimates of Model 1. All of the t-statistics are significant at the 10 per cent level or better, with the exception of the long-term structural constraint, ICOR.

The F test rejects the null hypothesis at the 1 per cent level, confirming that all the explanatory variables are jointly significant. The condition index shows no sign of serious multicollinearity, as was the case with the prior models. First-order autocorrelation is likely since the Durbin-Watson test is insignificant at the 1 per cent level.

Table 6.9 Weighted Least Squares Linear Probability Model, 1971–1981

Rescheduling Demand Indicators	Model 4 (First-order approximation) Coefficient	T-statistic	Model 5 (Second-order approximation) Coefficient	T-statistic
A. Rescheduling Mode Attributes				
Debt-service cost	0.0001	1.36	0.0007	4.28
Rescheduling cost	−0.001	−1.75	−0.005	−2.53
[Rescheduling cost]^2	n.a.	n.a.	0.0001	2.28
Rescheduling state	0.033	2.85	0.025	2.24
B Budget constraint characteristics				
Long-term structural	0.0009	1.01	0.005	2.53
[Long-term structural]^2	n.a.	n.a.	−0.00005	−2.08
Medium-term adjustment	0.111	3.28	0.099	2.95
Short-term liquidity	0.007	4.53	0.020	7.42
[Short-term liquidity]^2	n.a	n.a.	−0.0002	−5.70
Intercept	−0.045	−0.96	−0.037	−0.62
Adjusted R^2	.09		.15	
F-statistic	11.41		12.53	
Durbin–Watson statistic	1.20		1.27	
Maximum condition index	9.56		18.73	

The goodness-of-fit results are ambiguous when compared to those in Model 1. While the multiple correlation coefficient is considerably lower than that obtained from the ordinary least squares estimator, the historical classification efficiency is improved (see Table 6.7 on p. 112). Since the predicted probabilities are not necessarily contained within the unit interval for the modified least squares model, the out-of-sample error rates are not as efficient as those of Model 1.

This modified generalized least squares estimator was also applied to the specification which includes the second-order Taylor expansion variables. The results can be seen in Table 6.9 as Model 5. As expected, Model 5 produces a better fit of the data than does Model 4; all the coefficients are significant at the 2.5 per cent level or better. The signs of the second-order terms support the conclusions drawn from Model 2 concerning rescheduling demand behaviour.

6.7 Logit Probability Model

Due to its attractive threshold property, the logit probability model (a non-linear functional form) was also tested. Two separate specifications are examined. Model 6 includes only linear terms while Model 7 adds the quadratic variables tested in the linear probability model (that is, Models 2 and 5). A maximum likelihood estimator was used to generate the coefficients for both models (see Table 6.10). The results from both specifications support *a priori* theoretical expectations. All the coefficients are significant at the 10 per cent level or better, and the signs of the coefficients confirm the results of the linear models. The likelihood ratio statistic, which is distributed as chi-squared, rejects the null hypothesis that all coefficients are zero at the 0.5 per cent level.

Virtually all the goodness-of-fit measures for the two logit models are better than the results from the linear probability models. For the logit models, an analogous measure of the adjusted R^2 statistic is defined as the difference between unity and the likelihood ratio. This statistic is 29.7 per cent and 40.8 per cent for the linear and quadratic logit models, respectively. Thus, by this measure, the goodness of fit is improved vis-à-vis the results of the linear models. Only the fixed effects linear specification had a higher correlation coefficient.

The within-sample and out-of-sample classification efficiency of Model 6 is slightly better than the error rates obtained from the first-order linear probability Model 1. The quadratic logit model shows higher classification efficiency within sample than does the quadratic linear probability model. However, the quadratic linear probability model is a better out-of-sample predictor.

Table 6.10 Maximum Likelihood Logit Probability Model, 1971–1981

Rescheduling-Demand Indicators	Model 6		Model 7	
	Coefficient	Asymptotic T-statistic	Coefficient	Asymptotic T-statistic
A. *Rescheduling mode attributes*				
Debt-service cost	0.011	1.56	0.014	1.61
Rescheduling cost	−0.020	1.95	−0.063	2.42
[Rescheduling cost]²	n.a.	n.a.	0.0006	1.85
Rescheduling state	0.235	2.37	0.137	1.37
B. *Budget-constraint characteristics*				
Long-term structural	0.012	1.33	0.073	2.52
[Long-term structural]²	n.a.	n.a.	−0.0008	1.58
Medium-term adjustment	0.701	2.60	0.622	2.14
Short-term liquidity	0.052	3.47	0.239	6.13
[Short-term liquidity]²	n.a.	n.a.	−0.004	4.11
Intercept	−3.17	−6.12	−3.72	5.37
Adjusted R²	29.7		40.8	
−2Log Likelihood	359.23		321.41	

6.8 Conclusions

Table 6.11 presents the parameter estimates and the goodness-of-fit measures for the quadratic specification of the logit model, the weighted least squares and the ordinary least squares linear probability models, and the ordinary least squares fixed effects model. Amemiya (1981) recommends a direct comparison of the parameter estimates after adjusting the coefficients of the linear probability models by a conversion formula. An alternative approach is simply to compare the relative magnitudes or ordering of each model's coefficients.

The relative size or ordering of the estimated parameters in all three versions of the linear probability model are identical (see Table 6.11). The ranking of the coefficients in the logit model broadly supports the results of the linear probability models.[13]

For the average country in this sample it appears that exchange rate policy, as measured by the medium-term budget constraint, was the single most important explanatory variable during the 1970s and early 1980s. Clearly, an overvalued real exchange rate significantly increased a debtor's probability of debt rescheduling. The level of the purchasing power parity index had an average marginal impact on rescheduling probability over four times as great as the second most important variable: the rescheduling state (that is, prior rescheduling experience).

The rescheduling state variable acts as a proxy for all unspecified determinants of rescheduling behaviour. In particular, it is likely to incorporate at least two effects. First, inadequate debt service relief from prior reschedulings would increase the likelihood of successive (or correlated) debt agreements. Secondly, the incidence of prior debt reschedulings affects perceived, as well as actual, creditworthiness. Since the international creditors' assessment of a country's creditworthiness is a central element of ongoing credit supply, this indicator also measures the supply-side constraint to debt rescheduling behaviour.

The parameter estimates of the rescheduling state variable in the linear probability model range from being 25 per cent to 380 per cent larger than the third most influential variable: the short-term liquidity constraint. The logit model reverses the importance of these two variables. It shows that the level of external debt to international currency reserves has 74 per cent more influence on rescheduling behaviour than does prior rescheduling experience. Whatever the relative importance of these two variables, a higher level of net foreign liabilities directly raises a debtor's rescheduling probability.

Rescheduling cost (that is, imports to Gross Domestic Product)

Table 6.11 Comparison of the Logit and Linear Probability Models, 1971–1981

Rescheduling Demand Indicators	Model 6 (MLE 2nd-order logit)	Model 5 (WLS 2nd-order LPM)	Model 3 (OLS fixed-effects LPM)	Model 2 (OLS 2nd-order LPM)
A. *Rescheduling mode attributes*				
Debt-service cost	0.014	0.0007	0.0003	−0.0002 [b]
Rescheduling cost	−0.063	−0.005	−0.004[b]	−0.008
[Rescheduling cost]^2	0.0006	0.0001	0.00003[b]	0.0001
Rescheduling state	0.137	0.025	0.0236	0.077
B. *Budget constraint characteristics*				
Long-term structural	0.073	0.005	0.0007[b]	0.005
[Long-term structural]^2	−0.0008	−0.00005	−0.000005[b]	−0.00005
Medium-term adjustment	0.622	0.088	0.095	0.092
Short-term liquidity	0.239	0.020	0.015	0.016
[Short-term liquidity]^2	−0.004	−0.0002	−0.00008	−0.0001
Intercept	−3.72	−0.037[b]	—	−0.003[b]
Adjusted R^2	41	15	40	23
Combined error rates[a]				
Within sample	51	61	44	52
Out of sample	65	68	—	57

Notes
[a] The Type I and Type II classification error rates are considered to be equally costly and thus are weighted equally in combination.
[b] Does not meet the 10 per cent test for significance.

and the long-term structural constraint (or the incremental capital-output ratio, ICOR) have similarly sized elasticities. The marginal effect of these two variables on rescheduling probability is only one-fourth the impact from the short-term liquidity constraint. Despite the smaller marginal impact of these two variables on rescheduling behaviour, they are important factors.

The negative correlation between rescheduling probability and the ratio of imports to GDP is evidence that higher imports act as a disincentive to rescheduling. This is because the debtor recognizes that an important attendant cost of rescheduling is foregone imports (that is, real resources for development) resulting from the restricted credit supply. The positive coefficient for ICOR indicates that greater efficiency of resource use, particularly in the process of capital formation, significantly lowers the debt rescheduling probability.

The second choice-mode attribute – debt service cost – has only 10 per cent of the marginal impact which the first choice-mode – rescheduling cost – has on rescheduling probability. Hence, the increase in a country's rescheduling probability resulting from a 40 per cent rise in the debt service cost variable can be neutralized by a corresponding 10 per cent increase in imports to GDP.

The quadratic terms have a miniscule, albeit significant, impact on rescheduling probability. In all of the model specifications, each of these coefficients has a sign which is opposite to the corresponding first-order term. This confirms that the impact of each of the respective variables has a diminishing marginal impact on rescheduling behaviour.

The overall results of these models indicate that all six of the first-order explanatory variables are significant determinants of a debtor's rescheduling behaviour. For the models shown in Table 6.11, the ordering of the first-order explanatory variables suggests that the long-term structural budget constraint (marginal efficiency of capital) and the two 'prices' of the non-rescheduling and rescheduling choice modes (that is, debt-service cost and rescheduling cost, respectively) have the smallest marginal impact on rescheduling probability. Thus, the ICOR, COST, and MGDP variables are less important than the medium-term and short-term budget constraints, and the prior rescheduling experience of the debtor (that is, purchasing power parity index, debt-to-reserves and rescheduling state dependence, respectively).

The proxy variable for the debtor's medium-term stabilization policy (PPP) had the largest marginal impact on sovereign debt-service capacity. Short-term liquidity management of the stock of net foreign-exchange liabilities was also a very important determinant of rescheduling demand. A strong positive rescheduling state dependence was detected in the data, implying that access to external credit or other supply-side factors are as important as demand-side determinants of rescheduling behaviour.

For this sample of sixty-seven countries from 1971 to 1984, inefficient investment performance and the relative price of sustainable borrowing (debt service payments) versus the price of rescheduling (foregone imports) were factors with a small, albeit significant, influence on comparative sovereign debt-rescheduling behaviour.

The key determinants of sovereign rescheduling behaviour for this sample were insufficient adjustment of the real exchange rate in response to balance of payments shocks, poor foreign exchange asset-liability management and correlated reschedulings (perhaps reflecting a credit supply constraint or inadequate debt relief).

End-Chapter Notes

1   The rescheduling points were constructed primarily from IMF publications, 1981a, 1983a, 1985b, although other sources such as Bitterman, 1973; Hardy, 1982; Mendelson, 1983; OECD, 1979b; OECD, 1982; and the *Wall Street Journal*, various issues, were also used on a supplemental basis.

2   The structural constraint (ICOR) and the adjustment constraint (PPP) are computed as five-year and three-year moving averages, respectively. Hence, the 'raw' sample size used to compute the rescheduling indicators actually covers the time period 1966 to 1984. The rescheduling 'state' variable is the sum of the prior values of the dependent variable, beginning in 1970. With the exception of the debt service cost indicator which is contemporaneously specified, all the rest of the explanatory variables are lagged one year vis-à-vis the rescheduling observation.

3   All centrally planned economies are excluded due to the unavailability of key data. The methodology is easily adapted to this group, however, and offers interesting research possibilities. See Grossman and Solberg, 1983 for a creditworthiness assessment of the Soviet Union using cash flow sensitivity analysis.

4   As postulated in Chapter 5, a lower level of imports to GDP reduces the perceived cost of rescheduling which raises its likelihood. In certain cases, however, it is possible that the lower value of MGDP could reflect a foreign exchange shortage resulting from a prior rescheduling. While this caveat is plausible, the positive correlation between the rescheduling state variable (that is, the sum of past rescheduling observations) and MGDP shown in Table 6.6 would seem to contradict this interdependence.

5   This result supports a conclusion in Chapter 4 to reject the use of discriminant analysis as a credit-scoring technique for sovereign creditworthiness.

6   The multivariate tests for the equality of group means shown in Table 6.4 may not be accurate since these statistics assume equality of the dispersion matrices. Despite this restriction, certain studies have shown that results from a linear function can be quite robust in the face of significant multivariate group differences.

7   The results from principal component analysis of the liquidity, adjustment, and structural constraints to debt service capacity (not shown in the text) suggest that the variation of these indicators is mutually independent. Moreover, all the constraints are 'tighter' for the rescheduling group than for those of the non-rescheduling group. Each of the three constraints were positively correlated with the first three principal components of the total sample variance, respectively. Thus, each debt service capacity constraint is orthogonal to the other two budget constraints. Next the data was divided according to rescheduling and non-rescheduling groups, and the first three principal components were computed for each of the two groups. Each of the three constraints, while exhibiting positive correlation with one of the first three components for the non-rescheduling group, reversed their correlation and became strongly negatively correlated with each respective principal component for the rescheduling group. This opposite correlation suggests that each of the three budget constraints had changed significantly (that is, became 'binding') for the rescheduling group.

8   The *a priori* expectation concerning the sign of each coefficient permits a one-sided test for significance. Thus, t-statistics of 1.28, 1.65, 1.96, and 2.33 indicate that the coefficient is non-zero with a confidence level of 90 per cent, 95 per cent, 97.5 per cent and 99 per cent, respectively.

9   The condition indices are the square roots of the ratio of the largest standardized eigenvalue to each standardized individual eigenvalue. If the largest value exceeds 900, then serious multicollinearity exists which, in turn, is likely to produce unstable coefficients and high standard errors.

10 The test for first-order autocorrelation using the Durbin-Watson d statistic is biased upward towards 2 when a lagged dependent variable is used as an explanatory variable. Since the test statistic for Model 1 was able to reject the null hypothesis despite this bias (that is, the d statistic was below the lower bound), first-order autocorrelation is surely present in the model.

11 The adjusted R^2 statistic is an extremely poor measure of goodness of fit for the linear probability model. Only if the predicted probabilities are either exactly zero or one will a perfect fit be achieved. The interested reader should consult Morrison, 1972 for more on this issue. Due to the shortcomings of this statistic, another goodness-of-fit measure is used. By comparing the within-sample and out-of-sample predictive efficiency (the historical and prospective classification rates, respectively) of the model, a second goodness-of-fit measure is obtained.

12 Lacking any better methodology, the critical value or cut-off probability is chosen so as to minimize the cumulative sum of the Type

I and Type II error rates in each respective model. When the predicted rescheduling probability exceeds the cut-off value it is classified as a predicted rescheduling observation.

13 For the logit regression results (Models 6 and 7), the coefficients measure the explanatory variables' marginal effect on the log odds of rescheduling rather than on the rescheduling probability directly (as in the linear probability model).

7.
Predicted Creditworthiness and Portfolio Management

7.1 Introduction

Section 7.2 draws upon the findings of Chapter 6 to summarize briefly the broad movements in relative creditworthiness of major groups of countries during the period 1971–1984. The individual creditworthiness trends of sixteen developing countries that rescheduled at least twice during the 1970s are also examined to assess the usefulness of the quantitative credit-scoring models as a debt early warning system. Section 7.3 shows how the results of these models can be instrumental for efficient portfolio decisions, including the pricing of both new and non-performing international loans. Section 7.4 argues that the most efficient methodology for country risk analysis requires a quantitative credit scoring model used in conjunction with the structured qualitative approach (that is, analytical political and economic assessment). If used by both the debtors and creditors, it will help to encourage the renewed flow of investment capital to developing countries.

7.2 Predicted Trends in Sovereign Creditworthiness

Group Trends
Among the model specifications in Chapter 6 which can be used for forecasting, the logit model possessed the highest classification efficiency and proved to be the best fit for the sample data. This section uses the predicted rescheduling probabilities from logit Model 7 (see Table 6.10 on p. 122) to examine the trends of creditworthiness for both individual countries and certain broad groups during the period 1972–1984.

Average yearly rescheduling probabilities have been calculated for each group (that is, net oil exporting, high, middle and low income non-oil developing countries) which subdivided the sample for the Chow tests in Chapter 6. These results are presented graphically in Figure 7.1. The average rescheduling probability for the entire group shows a rising secular trend. Only in 1975, during the commodity price boom, and in 1984, amidst domestic austerity and resurgent exports (both of which narrowed the resource gap of the developing countries), did the average developing country rescheduling probability improve. The relative impact on these average probabilities from the first and second oil price shocks and other additional shocks originating from the developed countries (for example, growth slowdown, trade protectionism, rising real interest rates, exchange-rate volatility and deceleration of the growth rate of credit supply) can be identified.

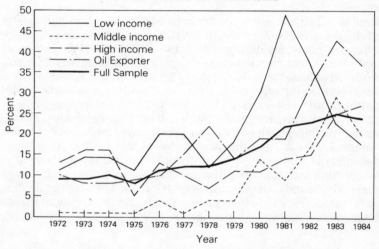

Figure 7.1   Average Country-group Rescheduling Probabilities

In 1978, the average rescheduling probability for all these developing countries stood 33.3 per cent higher than it did in 1972. The primary and secondary effects of the initial oil price shock clearly raised the probability of debt rescheduling and the risk of international lending, but the massive financial intermediation of the private international capital markets and the low initial indebtedness of the developing countries in 1972 maintained a fairly smooth recycling process during the 1970s. While average credit-worthiness declined, as shown by a higher average rescheduling probability (10–12 per cent), it did not immediately result in an increase in the incidence of rescheduling cases. Most rescheduling continued to involve middle or low income countries, many cases of which seemed to be chronic.[1] During the mid–1970s, the declining average creditworthiness of developing countries was not disruptive to the capital markets, nor was the growth trend of rescheduling probabilities unsustainable. Despite the deterioration in average creditworthiness in 1976 following the collapse of the commodity price bubble, average debt service capacity remained virtually stable during 1977 and 1978. Beginning in 1979, however, this stability was upset.

The second oil price shock in 1979 reduced the average debt service capacity of developing countries down further. The average rescheduling probability for this sixty-seven country sample stood at 17 per cent in 1980, 41.7 per cent higher than the level in 1978. Hence, given the already high levels of indebtedness, the second oil price shock was more damaging to average developing country creditworthiness over a shorter period of time than the first disturbance.

Not surprisingly, the third period, from 1980 to 1983, shows the most drastic deterioration in the average creditworthiness of the developing countries. Between 1980 and 1983, the average rescheduling probability of the sample increased by 47.1 per cent. The secondary effects of the second oil-price shock, combined with the contraction of new credit to developing countries and the change in monetary policy of the United States (which resulted in positive real interest rates and a rising dollar), all forcefully lowered average developing country creditworthiness. The confluence of these developments resulted in an unstable recycling process which dramatically increased the incidence of debt rescheduling (see Chapter 2 for a fuller account of these events).

Judged on the basis of the growth rates of the average debt rescheduling probabilities for the developing countries during these three periods, the events of 1981 to 1983 were the catalyst for the current debt crisis. It was the first and second oil price shocks, combined with inadequate developing country adjustment policies, which produced the high stock dependence of debtor countries on foreign capital. However, it was the secondary effects of the second oil-price increase, such as the synchronized OECD recession, new trade protectionism, the deflationary policy response of key industrialized countries (which hiked the real interest rates and raised the trade-weighted US dollar) and the collapse in the growth of international credit to developing countries which all resulted in the very sharp deterioration of developing country rescheduling probabilities.

Over the full fourteen-year period, the low income countries have the highest average rescheduling probability. This supports the assessment which the private credit markets made during the 1970s that this group possessed the poorest sovereign credit risk.

Low levels of development, structural rigidities in the economy and limited managerial expertise all tended to limit the ability of these countries to adjust effectively to external shocks. As shown in Figure 7.1 on p. 130, the average rescheduling probability of this group rose precipitously in the wake of the two oil price shocks and their ensuing secondary effects. These countries had to resort primarily to bilateral and multilateral credits (which incorporate a substantial grant element), due to the inability of these countries to tap the private capital markets. Despite the concessional credits, these countries were unable to avoid a significant number of debt reschedulings.[2]

By contrast, the middle income countries show the best average sovereign credit risk throughout the sample period. Until 1979, this group, compared to the other three groups in the sample, was on average unequivocally the most creditworthy. Beginning in 1978, however, this group's position deteriorated relative to the high income developing countries in particular. This may have been due to its lesser ability (compared to the high income debtors) to continue to finance imports, resulting in an externally imposed credit constrained stabilization. By forcing a reduction of imports, the external credit squeeze raised the relative price of sustained borrowing by lowering the disincentive to reschedule.[3]

The average rescheduling probability of the middle income countries rose faster than that of the overall sample between 1981 and 1983. This may have been due to the fact that the middle income countries, relying largely on non-manufactured commodities for export revenue, were not able to benefit greatly from the OECD recovery. Given the tight money recession and the industrial country recovery occurring in more non-traditional sectors, demand and thus prices for the traditional export products of these debtors remained weak. While the low-income countries also faced these same trade problems, their debt service ratios were lower (due to the relative absence of commercial debt) and their access to new concessional credit was better, both of which would tend to lower their rescheduling probability. Despite the deterioration of their creditworthiness after 1978, the middle income countries contributed the lowest proportion of reschedulings, amounting to an average of 1.0 per country during the period 1971–1984.

The rescheduling probabilities of the high income developing countries and the net-oil exporters over the fourteen-year period generally lie between the middle and low income groups and, on average, are quite similar. Although their full period averages are similar, their respective year to year movements are markedly different.

The creditworthiness of the high income countries declined from

1972 to 1974 as a result of the higher oil prices and the ensuing global recession which significantly widened this group's resource gap and increased its debt accumulation. The average creditworthiness of this group improved from 1975 to 1978, benefiting unequivocally from lower real oil prices, negative real interest rates on international credit and the renewed growth of world trade.

However, this improving trend in the rescheduling probability of high income debtors reversed itself with the second oil shock in 1979, putting this group on a new secular trend of declining creditworthiness which has yet to change. Their large debt level, much of which is subject to floating-rate interest payments, meant that higher global real interest rates produced significantly higher foreign exchange liability flows in the form of debt service payments. Tighter monetary policy in the United States which was transmitted globally also meant that some investment projects which had been financed with the expectation of low nominal or negative real interest rates were then insolvent. The inflationary impulse of higher oil prices, combined with inadequate downward flexibility in the nominal exchange rate, led to overvalued currencies and declining trade performance.[4] The confluence of these shocks after 1980 seems to have more than neutralized the beneficial effect of lower oil prices on average creditworthiness. This group had the highest proportion of reschedulings, averaging 2.0 per debtor during the entire sample period.

Movement in the average rescheduling probabilities of the net-oil exporting countries is negatively correlated with the trend in real oil prices. In 1974, the average rescheduling probability of the net oil exporters stood below its average rate in 1972. During the ensuing period when real oil prices declined, this group's rescheduling prospects increased concomitantly. The average rescheduling probability rose from 9 per cent in 1975 to a peak of 22 per cent in 1978. In 1979, the second oil price shock temporarily improved the average rescheduling probability of this group, but it deteriorated again in 1981.[5] This group had the second highest proportion of rescheduling, amounting to an average of 1.9 per debtor. This high incidence of debt rescheduling supports the thesis that unbridled lending (that is, an extremely elastic credit supply) to newly found, seemingly creditworthy, clients is ill advised. Kindleberger (1981) labels this phenomenon 'boom lending'. Such financial bubbles ultimately collapse when the growth of the supply of credit becomes inelastic.

The estimated rescheduling probabilities from Model 7 shown in Figure 7.1 generally support *a priori* expectations concerning the trends in relative creditworthiness for these four broad country classifications. Although the international lender can use these results to determine the covariance of risk among country groups (and to adjust the loan portfolio to minimize non-systematic risk), individual trends concerning sovereign rescheduling probability also are required.

Individual Debtor Trends and Country Lending Targets

Using the individual country results from Model 7, the actual and predicted rescheduling behaviour for selected developing countries are presented in Table 7.1. Each of the sixteen countries listed in Table 7.1 have rescheduled at least twice during the fourteen-year period in this sample. In Table 7.1 there are three columns associated with each debtor country. Y refers to the observed rescheduling behaviour of the country, where 0 signifies a non-rescheduling year and 1 represents a rescheduling observation. $\hat{Y}$ represents the country's rescheduling probability in each year as estimated by logit Model 7. The third column (R), presents the percentile ranking of the country for any given year vis-à-vis the other sixty-six countries in the sample.[6] For example, a percentile rank of 90 means the country's creditworthiness was in the 90th percentile, or its estimated debt service capacity exceeded 90 per cent of the sample. Similarly, if a country's rank equals 0, then it represents the poorest credit risk in the sample.

The $\hat{Y}$ statistic and the R statistic offer two different measures of an individual country's creditworthiness. For any given year, $\hat{Y}$ offers a cardinal or absolute measure of a country's creditworthiness. It states a country will reschedule with X per cent probability in any given year. As outlined in Chapter 3, the point estimate for rescheduling probability can be used either as an absolute measure of the likelihood of rescheduling in any given year (that is, *discrete absolute creditworthiness*) or as a measure of the country's trend vis-à-vis itself over time (that is, *dynamic absolute creditworthiness*).

For example, as seen in Table 7.1, the estimated rescheduling probabilities for Morocco were quite small between 1971 and 1978. Beginning in 1979, however, the projected rescheduling probabilities rose, culminating in a rescheduling in 1983 and 1984. In this case, the dynamic absolute creditworthiness was a good early warning indicator of its deteriorating debt service capacity.[7]

Not only was the declining trend apparent but the projected rescheduling probability in 1982 was high in absolute terms, thus alerting the creditor to the extraordinary risk. Since the sharp deterioration in Morocco's debt service capacity was quite evident as many as three to four years before it actually rescheduled, the astute creditor would have had plenty of time to lower exposure before arrears occurred.

The R statistic offers a comparative or ordinal assessment of a country's creditworthiness. As with the cardinal measure, this statistic can be used either in a discrete or in a dynamic manner. The country's relative position or rank amongst all the debtors in any given year produces its *discrete cross-sectional creditworthiness*. This measure would allow a creditor to identify and exclude the lowest quartile (or any proportion depending on the lender's risk averseness) from country limit increases and new lending.

Looking at the country's relative ranking or percentile over time, reveals its *dynamic cross-sectional creditworthiness*. In the case of Morocco, the value of the R statistic also supports the conclusion drawn from $\hat{Y}$. Beginning in 1978, Morocco's ranking amongst the sixty-seven country sample exhibited a secular decline, revealing its deteriorating performance relative to the changing group mean. Thus, not only was Morocco's creditworthiness declining relative to its own historical performance, it also was deteriorating relative to the declining average of other countries after 1977.

The results of the two creditworthiness measures do not always lead to similar conclusions. For example, from 1977 to 1980, the dynamic absolute creditworthiness measure ($\hat{Y}$) for Yugoslavia steadily worsened from 7 per cent in 1977 to 10 per cent in 1979. During the same time period, however, its percentile ranking or dynamic cross-sectional measure moved from 53 to 50 and then back to 55 in 1979. In this case the dynamic absolute measure of creditworthiness was a better early warning indicator than the percentile country ranking, since Yugoslavia encountered financial difficulties in 1980.

However, in certain cases the dynamic cross-sectional measure (or percentile) is more efficient than the dynamic absolute rescheduling measure. From 1974 to 1976, Sierra Leone's projected rescheduling probability remained constant at 5 per cent. During the same period its percentile score fell from 69 to 54, indicating that its relative position vis-à-vis the sixty-seven country group was deteriorating. Since Sierra Leone rescheduled its debt in 1977, the dynamic cross-sectional ranking was more accurate in this case.

Despite these two examples where the two dynamic measures yield disparate results, both generally are consistent with each other and quite indicative of imminent rescheduling problems. For most cases shown in Table 7.1, both $\hat{Y}$ and R deteriorate one to two years prior to an actual rescheduling observation. A one-year lead time (which is currently built into the model) allows a creditor institution significant opportunity to adjust its portfolio to minimize expected losses. In many cases the model will highlight a problem country even earlier than one year, allowing even more scope to lower medium-term risk exposure.

Table 7.1 Actual and Predicted Rescheduling Demand for Selected Debtor Countries, 1971–1984

Year	Argentina			Brazil			Chile			Costa Rica			Egypt			Ghana			Guyana			India		
	Y	Ŷ	R	Y	Ŷ	R	Y	Ŷ	R	Y	Ŷ	R	Y	Ŷ	R	Y	Ŷ	R	Y	Ŷ	R	Y	Ŷ	R
1971	0	16	19	0	15	22	1	67	2	0	8	37	1	20	9	0	7	42	0	4	85	1	43	4
1972	0	29	4	0	12	24	1	21	5	0	6	49	1	*	*	1	9	33	0	4	70	1	24	3
1973	0	28	7	0	10	27	1	39	2	0	6	53	0	46	2	0	7	48	0	6	55	1	24	6
1974	0	28	3	0	9	29	1	69	0	0	7	34	0	22	5	1	6	49	0	5	67	1	29	5
1975	0	36	5	0	15	10	1	89	0	0	7	41	0	16	15	0	10	29	0	14	12	1	35	0
1976	1	34	7	0	14	20	0	83	0	0	8	43	1	24	13	0	6	63	0	4	76	1	49	2
1977	0	13	25	0	15	18	0	30	10	0	7	55	0	34	9	0	12	27	0	4	80	1	53	4
1978	0	13	40	0	16	18	0	35	7	0	8	57	0	37	9	0	20	24	0	23	14	1	43	2
1979	0	17	33	0	52	0	0	50	2	0	10	53	0	38	11	0	*	*	0	26	16	0	43	3
1980	0	20	35	0	64	0	0	37	13	0	15	46	0	37	17	0	*	*	1	14	50	0	55	2
1981	0	31	26	0	62	7	0	46	13	1	17	45	0	22	34	0	*	*	1	50	9	0	*	*
1982	0	27	39	0	42	15	0	38	21	0	18	51	0	18	49	0	68	6	1	80	2	0	33	24
1983	1	22	35	1	44	14	1	30	33	1	17	50	0	31	30	0	*	*	1	92	1	0	31	28
1984	1	*	*	1	68	8	1	26	33	1	*	*	0	33	20	0	*	*	1	95	0	0	*	*

Year	Jamaica			Liberia			Mexico			Morocco			Peru			Sierra Leone			Yugoslavia			Zambia		
	Y	$\hat{Y}$	R	Y	$\hat{Y}$	R	Y	$\hat{Y}$	R	Y	$\hat{Y}$	R	Y	$\hat{Y}$	R	Y	$\hat{Y}$	R	Y	$\hat{Y}$	R	Y	$\hat{Y}$	R
1971	0	3	90	0	*	*	0	11	27	0	4	87	0	5	60	0	2	94	1	20	7	0	2	96
1972	0	3	93	0	*	*	0	10	26	0	5	56	1	6	51	0	3	85	0	16	9	0	2	98
1973	0	3	86	0	*	*	0	12	17	0	8	40	0	7	47	0	4	75	0	8	40	0	11	20
1974	0	4	83	0	*	*	0	12	19	0	7	45	0	11	19	0	5	69	0	7	37	0	23	9
1975	0	6	39	0	*	*	0	14	17	0	6	59	0	11	24	0	5	68	0	5	58	0	17	9
1976	0	5	68	0	8	39	1	19	14	0	5	61	1	6	37	1	5	54	0	9	38	0	23	10
1977	0	5	70	0	7	46	0	35	5	0	6	61	0	12	20	1	7	52	0	7	53	0	28	11
1978	1	42	4	0	9	41	0	43	5	0	6	59	1	26	13	0	6	57	0	9	50	0	14	21
1979	1	33	13	0	13	36	0	49	6	0	12	41	0	23	17	1	11	47	0	10	55	0	33	14
1980	1	45	7	1	15	44	0	30	22	0	18	29	1	29	16	1	17	31	1	26	28	0	31	15
1981	1	44	15	1	17	43	0	33	23	0	29	24	0	11	57	0	12	48	0	*	*	0	30	19
1982	0	31	28	1	18	40	1	31	26	0	46	13	0	25	30	0	18	38	0	35	22	0	17	43
1983	1	47	10	1	88	2	1	93	0	1	73	4	1	23	45	0	38	20	1	65	10	1	31	29
1984	1	*	*	1	73	3	1	93	1	1	72	5	1	31	23	1	*	*	1	70	6	1	11	65

Key:

Y = actual rescheduling behaviour where 0 = non-rescheduling and 1 = rescheduling.

$\hat{Y}$ = predicted rescheduling probability using the logit probability Model 7 (see Table 6.10).

R = percentile ranking amongst the sample of sixty-seven countries (for example, R = 10 means that the country is more creditworthy than 10 per cent of the debtors.

* = missing data.

In order to utilize the model's predicted rescheduling probabilities to set individual country limits, the discrete cross-sectional creditworthiness measure is preferable to the discrete absolute creditworthiness interpretation.[8] Rather than categorizing the entire sample into rescheduling and non-rescheduling candidates in any given year (as in the discrete absolute method), a percentile ranking based on the predicted rescheduling probabilities ($\hat{Y}$) allows the creditor a more accurate first cut at risk management. Since certain countries will reschedule when $\hat{Y}$ is quite small (for example, Sierra Leone, 1977), while others will not reschedule even when $\hat{Y}$ is quite large (for example, India, 1980), a global critical value used to classify $\hat{Y}$ into rescheduling versus non-rescheduling groups would be quite inaccurate.

Once the first cut has been made using the discrete cross-sectional method, then each individual country's dynamic absolute creditworthiness should be assessed using Z scores. If a debtor's predicted rescheduling probability deteriorates significantly relative to its own history, then it should be classified as a high risk country, even if it has a low rescheduling probability relative to the rest of the portfolio. Similarly, if a country's dynamic cross-sectional creditworthiness reveals that its prospects are deteriorating relative to the group, then it also should be considered risky even if its predicted absolute rescheduling probability is low. These second and third cuts at the data will allow the minimization of Type I error rates or false non-rescheduling predictions.

In order to minimize Type II error rates or false rescheduling predictions, which result in foregone business opportunities, the countries deemed uncreditworthy according to the first cut should be assessed a second time using the dynamic methods. If the debtor's dynamic creditworthiness, measured either cardinally or ordinally, shows an improving trend, then new business should be contemplated. Clearly in this case, some uncertainty will remain so that the degree of the creditor's risk aversion must be weighed against the higher nominal returns on the asset.[9]

The model is used most effectively when the relative cross-sectional measure is used to divide the entire developing country debtors into likely versus unlikely rescheduling candidates. Next the division can be finely tuned by applying the dynamic absolute and cross-sectional measures of creditworthiness. Used in this manner, the results shown in Table 7.1 on p. 136 are both extremely meaningful and directly operational for an international creditor attempting to differentiate sovereign creditworthiness and set country lending targets.

7.3 Portfolio Theory and Capital Markets

Credit-Scoring Models and Portfolio Management

Arrears on debt-service payments, an involuntary refinancing, concessional rescheduling, or debt repudiation all represent varying degrees of erosion of commercial bank profitability. The chief credit officer responsible for a commercial bank's international portfolio must incorporate, country by country, the expected likelihood of each of these eventualities along with the nominal rate of return for each asset in setting individual country targets and managing the overall portfolio. The portfolio of international assets can be managed either by maximizing the expected rate of return on the portfolio subject to a given level of risk, or the risk can be minimized subject to a given rate of return.[10]

The expected value of a loan portfolio is simply the weighted average of the expected values of each loan where the respective weights are the size of each individual loan relative to the entire portfolio. The variance of the portfolio or its overall risk is determined not only by the standard deviation of the rate of return for each asset but also by the correlation coefficient for each pair of assets. In other words, the risk of the portfolio is affected not only by the variation of the rate of return for each asset but also by the manner in which the rates of return for two or more assets move together.

Portfolio theory contends that the overall risk associated with any 'bundle' of assets, which in this case is a group of international loans, can be separated into non-systematic and systematic components (Modigliani and Pogue, 1974). Assuming that the rates of return of all assets are not perfectly correlated, then by diversifying the mix of assets the non-systematic portion of risk can be lowered or possibly even removed from the loan portfolio altogether. Hence the variance or riskiness of the portfolio is lowered and an efficient portfolio (minimum risk) is achieved.

Non-systematic risk is asset specific since it is determined by the individual debtor country's economic, financial and political performance. Each debtor possesses a degree of non-systematic risk which uniquely determines a portion of its overall rescheduling probability and hence the overall variance of the rate of return on its loans (as viewed from the perspective of the lender). The portion of non-systematic risk to overall risk will vary by country and will be independent of the rescheduling probabilities of all other countries (or of the rates of return on other assets).

Systematic risk represents underlying factors which commonly affect the rescheduling probability of all individual debtors. Typically, these factors would result from a variety of exogenous economic disturbances (for example, interest rate movements, changes in global liquidity, or the growth of world trade). Hence, the systematic risk of any debtor country is that portion of its total risk which is common to all debtors (or assets). While each asset or country will be affected to differing degrees by systematic risk, it will persist despite portfolio diversification. Therefore, an efficient portfolio strategy would alter relative country exposure after measuring the impact of this economic disturbance on both the expected returns for each particular asset and its effect on the overall riskiness or variance on the return of the bank's international loan portfolio.

In order to construct an efficient international portfolio, a credit manager must compute the present value of the risk-adjusted future stream of earnings, either from each individual asset or from the average return on assets for a particular debtor. This will require a schedule of future payments associated with the asset (or assets), a forecast of a risk-free interest rate for each period, the likelihood of repayment during each period and a country-specific risk premium.[11]

The predicted rescheduling probabilities, $\hat{Y}$, from the credit-scoring models presented in Chapter 6 can be used to determine this expected payoff probability, $(1-\hat{Y})$. The scheduled income from the asset during each future period (for example, interest payments, fee income and other perceived quantifiable benefits) can be weighted by the predicted likelihood of sustained borrowing or non-rescheduling probability $(1 - \hat{Y})$. The entire portfolio's expected return is simply the weighted average of the expected return from each individual asset (or country), where the weights equal the proportion of each asset's value to the value of the entire portfolio.

The individual country risk premium reflects the estimated variance of the rate of return on the loan to each debtor country and its interaction with the variance of the rate of return for the bank's entire international portfolio. The credit-scoring models presented in Chapter 6 can also be used to determine this statistic.[12] On the assumption that the correlation coefficient is not unity, then portfolio diversification becomes a robust means of minimizing the variance or risk in the portfolio of international assets. The purpose of the credit-scoring models developed in this study is to contribute objectively determined values of $\hat{Y}$ which can be used directly to efficiently manage a portfolio of international assets by minimizing non-systematic risk.

The efficiency of portfolio diversification is dependent fundamentally upon the robustness of the credit-scoring model in distinguishing problem debtors from creditworthy borrowers. However, any credit assessment involves the potential for a Type I error (false non-rescheduling prediction) or a Type II error (false rescheduling prediction). Commercial banks would prefer to avoid Type II errors inasmuch as they represent foregone business opportunities which would have encompassed acceptable risks and meant additional profit. Type I errors, which imply non-performing loans with varying degrees of erosion to bank earnings, and under severe cases even its capital base, represent an even greater cost. Therefore, since banks would probably attribute a higher cost to Type I errors, thereby raising the incidence of Type II errors, there is a fear on the part of bank regulators that the widespread use of credit-scoring models will unduly restrict capital access to a portion of otherwise creditworthy borrowers (the Type II error candidates). This, in turn, could lead to *de facto* debtor country illiquidity, and perhaps even insolvency, if market-based credit restriction forced an involuntary reduction of non-compressible imports for the debtor.

These fears are unwarranted for two reasons. First, it has been shown that sovereign debt rescheduling models can be reasonably efficient as a credit-scoring device. Used as one component of a comprehensive sovereign credit-risk assessment system, overall error rates (both Type I and II) can be minimized. Thus, the use of sovereign credit-scoring models should help to renew lending to developing countries. Second, one of the responsibilities of a lender of last resort (such as the International Monetary Fund or other multilateral or bilateral agencies) is to ensure that countries which are likely candidates for a Type II error classification, do in fact receive sufficient capital inflows. Just as the profit-oriented banks were reticent to lend heavily to the low income countries during the 1970s, they would also resist lending heavily to debtors which are Type II error candidates. Since no credit-scoring system is perfect, Type II errors are bound to occur. This residual demand for international credit from the borderline creditworthy countries necessitates an additional role for the IMF, IBRD, or certain bilateral credit agencies.

The Pricing of International Assets
A perceived decline in a particular country's creditworthiness cannot always easily be followed by a reduction of the lender's loan exposure. Although changes in short-term exposure can be implemented fairly quickly, the 'lumpiness' of medium- and long-term international assets within a portfolio can hinder efficient marginal adjustments to shifts in perceived risk. The development since 1983 of a makeshift secondary market in international loan swaps (debt-for-debt, debt-for-equity, and debt-for-cash) thus, however, allows greater flexibility of action and further improves a manager's ability to make smooth portfolio adjustments. The rise of this market requires a lender to take an independent view on the pricing of these

assets, particularly those of a rescheduled borrower. The predicted rescheduling probabilities from the sovereign credit-scoring model can be used to discount accurately this loan paper for the secondary market.[13]

Assume that the interest rate charged on a sovereign loan equals the sum of the interest rate on a risk-free asset (e), and a country-specific risk premium (z), which reflects the borrower's relative riskiness. In a perfectly competitive market, a risk neutral lender will price an asset so that the risk premium will exactly compensate for the predicted rescheduling probability ($\hat{Y}$) associated with the asset.[14] According to these assumptions, the expected rate of return of the risky asset will exactly equal the rate of return of the risk-free asset. Equation 7.1 states this relationship algebraically.

$$(1 - \hat{Y})[1 + (e + z)] = 1 + e$$

Equation 7.1

Rearranging the terms in 7.1 to solve for the risk premium, z, Equation 7.2 is obtained.

$$z = [\hat{Y}/(1 - \hat{Y})][1 + e]$$

Equation 7.2

As the predicted rescheduling probability of the debtor rises, it is obvious that the risk premium increases. If only a portion of the scheduled debt service payment is actually paid (u) then 7.2 can be altered to account for this eventuality.[15] Equation 7.3 incorporates this element.

$$z = [u\hat{Y}/(1 - u\hat{Y})][1 + e]$$

Equation 7.3

Equation 7.3 can be extended to a multi-period model by making the rescheduling probability and the portion of debt service actually paid a function of time (t). This alteration yields Equation 7.4.

$$z = \sum_{t=1}^{T} \{[u(t)\hat{Y}(t)/(1 - u(t)\hat{Y}(t))][1 + e]\}/T$$

Equation 7.4

The risk premium is determined by an average of the discounted rescheduling probabilities for each year of the outstanding loan. With the estimated risk premium from Equation 7.4, the discounted price (p) of an impaired asset for a risk neutral lender can be calculated directly. Let the actual rate of return on an impaired asset, which is by definition less than the contractual rate of return, be denoted by v. The discount on the impaired asset equals the ratio of the current yield on the impaired asset to the equilibrium rate of return on the performing asset.

$$p = v/(e + z)$$

Equation 7.5

Computed in this manner, the discount ensures that the impaired asset's effective yield will be equal to the equilibrium rate of return. Notice that if the asset is truly non-performing (that is, there is zero return) then the asset is totally worthless. Alternatively, if the impaired asset is returning only 11 per cent when it should be returning 14 per cent, then it should be discounted 21.4 per cent (that is, priced at 78.6 per cent) in the marketplace. This technique can price an impaired asset for sale in the secondary market, identify arbitrage opportunities, or help to evaluate debt-for-equity swaps, among other applications.

7.4 International Lending and Country Risk Analysis

The heightened uncertainties in international financial relations since 1982 have raised the risk averseness of lenders which, in turn, has contributed to the marked deceleration of new lending to developing countries. Wider use of an efficient credit-scoring methodology, by minimizing the subjective element of judgment in current risk assessments, would reduce the prevailing uncertainty and contribute to the resolution of the current impasse in international financial intermediation.

Being able to identify the factors underlying debt-service payment arrears, whether due to liquidity, adjustment, or structural constraints or some combination thereof, should contribute to a smoother process of international lending. One of the problems associated with international lending, particularly after 1979, was a mismatch between the maturity structure of the sources and uses of external funds extended to the developing countries.

With the shift in risk preference on the part of private lenders after the second oil-price shock in 1979, the term structure of new lending was markedly shortened. Thus, the growth rate of short-term debt exceeded the growth rate of long-term debt during 1980 to 1982. At the same time, many developing countries did not sufficiently implement deflationary policies to compensate for the increased international 'tax' on national income caused by higher oil import expenditures. Hence, borrowing requirements rose for these countries with excess demand for investment and, in some cases, consumption. Funding long-term investment projects and shifts in inter-temporal consumption preferences with short-term debt is inappropriate. Once the point was reached in 1982 when the international capital markets would not roll over the short-term maturities, debtor countries had little alternative but to accumulate arrears and ultimately unilaterally request a debt rescheduling.

Since most private commercial banks are unwilling to lend money to developing countries for a term in excess of eight to ten years, this group of creditors should finance problems of illiquidity and trade adjustment rather than longer term solvency borrowing require-ments. Since the gestation period on development-related invest-ment projects is typically longer than the preferred term structure of private lenders, these capital requirements are best met by bilateral aid flows or IBRD project lending. Therefore commercial banks should be lending to illiquid, although solvent, borrowers, while the World Bank and bilateral agencies should be directing credit to insolvent debtor countries.

Financial intermediation will be improved and the market-induced incentives for debt rescheduling will be minimized:

(1) by easing the current constraint on new borrowing by developing countries;
(2) by better matching the maturity requirements of the sources and uses of funds, and;
(3) by avoiding perverse pricing policies whereby rescheduling countries obtain lower interest rates than creditworthy borrowers.

The wider application of quantitative credit-scoring models to assess relative sovereign risk and to determine the pricing for both new and impaired assets would help to achieve these policy goals.

Besides being useful for international financial intermediation, a quantitative credit-scoring model also can aid in the formulation of international macroeconomic and debt management policy for developing countries. Astute borrowers have directed foreign sav-ings into profitable domestic investment projects which produce tradable goods. They have also implemented timely balance of payments adjustment programmes and have actively managed their international liquidity balance. In most cases, these countries have managed to avoid the wrenching experience of arrears, debt rescheduling and IMF-imposed austerity. This suggests that a developing country should incorporate a debt early-warning system which uses proxy variables for these constraints into their planning process. Not only will use of this model allow a check on the financial sustainability of their economic plan, it will also indicate how such policies will be perceived by the international capital markets.

By focusing on the economic factors determining the debt service capacity of a developing country, the quantitative approach to country risk analysis has shown that it can be useful in a variety of applications. It is not meant, however, to be the sole tool of assessment for country risk analysis. A political assessment of sovereign risk is also crucial to obtain a comprehensive outlook for a debtor's creditworthiness. Currently, however, it is easier to incorporate a political assessment into a more traditional analysis which relies on qualitative judgements. Hence a quantitative credit-scoring model is not a substitute for the structured qualitative approach as outlined in Chapter 4. Rather, a quantitative credit-scoring model is complementary to the structured qualitative assessment. An in-depth qualitative assessment of a particular country facilitates a cardinal measure, while a quantitative assessment is best applied as an ordinal measure of creditworthiness. Taken together, these two systems of sovereign risk assessment represent the best combination for state-of-the-art country risk analysis.

End-Chapter Notes

1 Many of the countries that rescheduled their external debt during the period 1973–1978 were familiar with this exercise, having done so prior to 1973. It is likely that the increased incidence of rescheduling from 1973 to 1978 represented the same group of pre–1973 rescheduling countries whose creditors were increasing the grant element of lending (resource transfer).

2 The regression results for the low income countries alone showed that the relative price of the rescheduling versus non-rescheduling option was an important factor in debt rescheduling behaviour. Despite concessional rates, the price of sustained borrowing (measuring both current and future debt service costs) was higher than the price to reschedule (that is, imports to GDP). In addition, poor liquidity management as signified by a high level of net external liabilities (that is, foreign debt to international reserves), inadequate trade adjustment as evidenced by an overvalued currency and the incidence of past reschedulings were also shown to be especially important

factors in explaining the rescheduling behaviour of low income countries.

3   Regression results for the middle income countries alone show that imports to GDP or the opportunity cost of rescheduling was a particularly important variable. Thus, any erosion in their ability to fund imports from new external credits (as occurred increasingly after 1979) would have forced a reduction of imports and raised the incentive to reschedule according to the theory presented in Chapter 5.

4   In contrast to the low and middle income countries, price factors relating to the rescheduling or non-rescheduling choice were not particularly significant for the high income debtors. Nor was the prior experience of debt rescheduling an important indicator of current debt service capacity. It was the three budget constraints to creditworthiness, namely the long-term structural, medium-term adjustment and the short-term liquidity constraints which were the most significant. Thus, the debt rescheduling behaviour of the high income debtors can best be explained by: debt accumulation which was too rapid, insufficient balance of payments adjustment (particularly involving the real exchange rate) and an overly aggressive investment policy leading to a rising incremental capital-output ratio.

5   Like the high income countries, the oil exporting debtors suffered from the long-term structural budget constraint. Due to the plethora of foreign exchange, many oil exporters pursued an overly aggressive investment programme. A classic boom economy always results in a certain proportion of bad investment decisions owing to the associated euphoria and attendant physical bottlenecks. Aggressive investment leads to shortages of complementary investment or intermediate goods which will lengthen the average gestation period and raise the incremental capital-output ratio, thus lowering its rate of return. Interestingly, the medium-term adjustment constraint was not an especially significant variable for the oil exporters as a group. Thus 'Dutch disease' (i.e., the tendency of newly-discovered exportable natural resources to overvalue the currency and atrophy traditional export industries) was not a pervasive phenomenon for the oil exporters although certain countries did suffer from this problem. See Corden (1982) for a survey of this literature. The short-term budget constraint and the price of sustained borrowing were two other particularly significant variables in explaining the rescheduling behaviour of the net oil exporters.

6   The number of countries in the sample for any given year may not always equal sixty-seven due to missing observations.

7   In 1979 the Z-score revealed that the projected rescheduling probability was 3.7 standard deviations above the mean of all the preceding observations for Morocco. By 1982, the Z-score showed that Morocco's creditworthiness was deteriorating even faster since the projected rescheduling probability was 4.9 standard deviations above the mean of previous values.

8   The discrete absolute creditworthiness method was used in Chapter 6, as in other published studies, to compare the results of the different

models. This absolute scheme requires a cut-off probability above which the country-year prediction is classified as rescheduling and below which it is considered as non-rescheduling. Type I (false non-rescheduling prediction) and Type II (false rescheduling prediction) error rates are computed, using this formulation.

9 Once a logit equation has been estimated, it is possible to extend the time horizon of the forecasted rescheduling probability well beyond the one year lead time which is built into the models presented in this book. Another model can be used to project baseline and alternative values for the explanatory variables used in the logit model. Once future sets of explanatory variables are forecast for each individual debtor, the logit model will state the long-term debt rescheduling probability forecast for each debtor. In this manner a consistent set of forecasts allowing a sensitivity analysis of the rescheduling probability for any individual debtor is obtained.

10 If it is assumed that the utility-based decision process for banks can be approximated by a quadratic function, then managing the loan portfolio can be achieved by estimating the expected rate of return on the portfolio and the uncertainty associated with the expected return, or the variance of the portfolio. If quadratic utility cannot be assumed then the portfolio can be described only by examining higher moments of the skewed probability distribution (see Goodman, 1981).

11 See Walter, 1981; and Nadauld, 1981 for a detailed presentation of the methodology required to calculate the present value of an asset's uncertain future cash flow.

12 See Goodman, 1981 for one method of differentiating systematic versus non-systematic risk for a particular debtor country when data on rates of return are unavailable.

13 An analogous technique can be used to price new loans or bond issues for developing country borrowers.

14 This multi-period extension of a single period model of loan price determination presented by Edwards, 1983 was developed by Lee Ohanian and myself in 1986 as a background to some (unpublished) empirical work we conducted for Security Pacific National Bank.

15 Unless the unpaid portion of scheduled debt service payments $(1 - u)$ is repudiated, its postponement implies residual value. Treatment of this issue has been omitted from the text, however, the method of accounting for these residual payments is central to fine-tuning the model.

Bibliography

Alter, G. M. (1961), 'The servicing of foreign capital inflows by underdeveloped countries', in H. S. Ellis (ed.) *Economic Development for Latin America* (New York: St. Martin's Press), pp. 139–67.

Altman, E. I. (1980), 'Commercial bank lending: process, credit scoring, and costs of errors in lending', *Journal of Financial and Quantitative Analysis*, vol. 15, no. 4, pp. 813–32.

Amemiya, T. (1981), 'Qualitative response models: a survey', *Journal of Economic Literature*, vol. 19, no. 4, pp. 1483–1536.

Amin, S. (1976), *Unequal Development: An Essay on the Social Formations of Peripheral Capitalism*, (New York: Monthly Review Press).

Anderson, T. W. (1958), *An Introduction to Multivariate Statistical Analysis*, (New York: John Wiley and Sons).

Argy, V. (1981), *The Postwar International Money Crisis: An Analysis* (London: Allen & Unwin).

Avramovic, D., and Gulhati, R. (1958), *Debt Servicing Capacity and Post War Growth in International Indebtedness* (Baltimore, Md.: The John Hopkins Press).

Avramovic, D. *et al.* (1964), *Economic Growth and External Debt* (Baltimore, Md.: John Hopkins Press).

Balassa, B. (1980), 'The process of industrial development and alternative development strategies', Graham Memorial Lecture delivered at Princeton University, 17 April.

Bank for International Settlements (1983), 'International banking developments: second quarter 1983', Basle.

Belsley, D. A., Kuh, E., and Welsch, R. E. (1980), *Regression Diagnostics* (New York: John Wiley and Sons).

Bernstein, E. M. (1958), 'Strategic factors in balance of payments', *Review of Economics and Statistics*, February, pp. 133–42.

Bitterman, H. J. (1973), *The Refunding of International Debt* (Durham, NC: Duke University Press).

Chenery, H., and MacEwan, A. (1966), 'Optimal patterns of growth and aid: the case of Pakistan', in H. Chenery (ed.), *Structural Change and Development Policy* (New York: Oxford University Press), pp. 342–77.

Chenery, H., and Strout, A. (1966), 'Foreign assistance and economic development', *American Economic Review*, vol. 56, no. 4, pp. 679–733.

Chow, G. (1960), 'Tests of equality between sets of coefficients in two linear regressions', *Econometrica*, vol. 28, pp. 591–605.

Cizauskas, A. C. (1979), 'International debt renegotiation: lessons from the past", *World Development*, vol. 7, pp. 199–210.

Clifton, E. V. (1982), 'Debtor-creditor games: an approach to international debt renegotiations', Federal Reserve Bank of New York Research Paper no. 8232, New York.

Cline, W. R. (1983), 'International debt and the stability of the world economy', Institute for International Economics, Policy Analysis in International Economics no. 4, Washington, DC.

Cline, W. R. (1984), *International Debt: Systematic Risk and Policy Response* (Washington, DC: Institute For International Economics).

Collins, R. A., and Green, R. D. (1982), 'Statistical methods for bankruptcy forecasting', *Journal of Economics and Business*, vol. 34, pp. 349–54.

Corden, W. M. (1982), 'Booming sector and Dutch disease economies – a survey', Working paper no. 79 (Canberra: Australian National University), November.

Cox, D. R. (1970), *The Analysis of Binary Data* (London: Methuen & Co. Ltd).

Davis, R. R. (1981), 'Alternative techniques for country risk evaluation', *Business Economics*, vol. 16, no. 3, pp. 34–41.

DeVries, B. (1971), 'The debt bearing capacity of developing countries – a comparative analysis', *Banca Nazionale del Lavoro Quarterly Review*, March, pp. 65–88.

Dhonte, P. (1974), 'Quantitative indicators and analysis of external debt problems', International Monetary Fund mimeo, Washington, DC.

Dhonte, P. (1975), 'Describing External Debt Situations: A Roll-Over Approach', *IMF Staff Papers*, vol. 22, no. 1, pp. 159–86.

Dhonte, P. (1979), *Clockwork Debt* (Lexington, Mass.: D.C. Heath and Co.).

Domar, E. D. (1950), 'The effect of foreign investment on the balance of payments,' *American Economic Review*, vol. 40, pp. 805–26.

Domencich, T. A., and McFadden, D. (1975), *Urban Travel Demand: A Behavioral Analysis* (Amsterdam: North Holland).

Edwards, S. (1983), 'LDC foreign borrowing and default risk: an empirical investigation, 1976–80', Working paper no. 1172, National Bureau of Economic Research, July.

Efron, B. (1975) 'The efficiency of logistic regression compared to normal discriminant analysis', *Journal of the American Statistical Association*, vol. 70, pp. 892–98.

Eisenbeis, R. A. (1977), 'Pitfalls in the application of discriminant analysis in business, finance, and economics', Federal Deposit Insurance Corporation Research Paper no. 75, Washington, DC.

Eisenbeis, R. A., and Avery, R. B. (1972), *Discriminant Analysis and Classification Procedures: Theory and Applications* (Lexington, Mass.: D. C. Heath and Co.).

Emmanuel, A. (1972), *Unequal Exchange: An Essay on the Imperialism of Trade* (New York: Monthly Review Press).

Erbe, R. (1982), 'Foreign indebtedness and economic growth: The Philippines', *Intereconomics*, no. 3, pp. 125–32.

Erbe, R., and Schattner, S. (1980), 'Indicator systems for the assessment of the external debt situation of developing countries', *Intereconomics*, no. 6, pp. 285–89.

Export and Import Bank of the U.S. (1976), 'A survey of country evaluation systems in use', Washington, DC.

Faaland, J. (1967), 'Comments on Mr. Gulhati's paper', in J. H. Adler (ed.) *Capital Movements and Economic Development* (New York: St. Martin's Press), pp. 261–64.

Feder, G. (1978), 'Economic growth, foreign loans, and debt service capacity of developing countries', World Bank Staff Working Papers, no. 274, Washington, DC.

Feder, G. (1981), 'Growth and external borrowing in trade gap economies of less developed countries', *Aussenwirtschaft*, vol. 36, pp. 381–95.

Feder, G., and Just, R. (1976), 'A study of debt service capacity applying logit analysis', *Journal of Development Economics*, vol. 4, pp. 25–39.

Feder, G., Just, R., and Ross, K. (1981), 'Projecting Debt Service Capacity of Developing Countries', *Journal of Financial and Quantitative Analysis*, vol. 16, no. 5, pp. 651–69.

Fisk, C., and Rimlinger, F. (1979), 'Nonparametric estimates of LDC repayment prospects', Central Intelligence Agency mimeo, Washington, DC.

Frank, C. R., and Cline, W. R. (1971), 'Measurement of debt servicing capacity: an application of discriminant analysis', *Journal of International Economics*, vol. 1, pp. 327–44.

Freedman, C. (1977), 'The euro-dollar market – a review of five recent studies', *Journal of Monetary Economics*, vol. 3, pp. 467–78.

Freedman, D. (1981), 'Some pitfalls in large econometric models: a case study', *Journal of Business*, vol. 54, no. 3, pp. 479–500.

Friedman, I. (1983) *The World Debt Dilemma: Managing Country Risk* (Washington, DC: Council for International Banking Studies and Philadelphia: Robert Morris Associates).

Goldberger, A. S. (1964), *Econometric Theory* (New York: John Wiley and Sons).

Goodman, L. S. (1981), 'Bank lending to non-OPEC LDC's: are risks diversifiable?', in *Federal Reserve Bank of New York Quarterly Bulletin*, vol. 6, no. 2, pp. 10–20.

Goodman, S. (1977), 'How the big U.S. banks really evaluate sovereign risks', in *Euromoney*, February, pp. 105–10.

Grinols, E. (1976), 'International debt rescheduling and discrimination using financial variables', U.S. Treasury Department mimeo, Washington, DC.

Grossman, G., and Solberg, R. L. (1983), *The Soviet Union's Hard-Currency Balance of Payments and Creditworthiness in 1985* (Santa Monica, Calif.: The RAND Corp.)

Gulhati, R. (1967), 'The "need" for foreign resources, absorptive capacity and debt servicing capacity', in J. H. Adler (ed.) *Capital Movements and Economic Development* (New York: St. Martin's Press), pp. 240–60.

Gutentag, J. M., and Herring, R. J. (1983), 'Overexposure of international banks to country risk: diagnosis and remedies', testimony before the U.S. Congress, House Committee on Banking, Finance and Urban Affairs, Subcommittee on International Trade, Investment, and Monetary Policy, 98th Congress, April.

Haendel, D. (1979), *Foreign Investments and the Management of Political Risk* (Boulder, Colo: Westview Press).

Hallwood, P., and Sinclair, S. (1981), *Oil, Debt and Development: OPEC in the Third World* (London: George Allen & Unwin).

Halperin, M., Blackwelder, W. C., and Verter, J. I. (1971), 'Estimation of the multivariate logistic risk function: a comparison of the discriminant function and maximum likelihood approaches', *Journal of Chronic Diseases*, vol. 24, pp. 125–58.

Hardy, C. V. (1981), 'Rescheduling developing-country debts', *The Banker*, July, pp. 33–8.

Hardy, C. V. (1982), 'Rescheduling developing-country debts, 1956–1981: lessons and recommendations', Overseas Development Council monograph no. 15, Washington, DC.

Heertje, A., *et al.* (1984), *The U.S.A. in the World Economy* (San Francisco: Freeman, Cooper and Co).

Heller, R. H. (1980), 'Country risk and international portfolio management', presented at a conference on Managing Country Risk, New York, January.

Hurd, M. (1979), 'Estimation in truncated samples when there is heteroscedasticity', *Journal of Econometrics*, vol. 11, pp. 247–58.

Ingram, F. J., and Frazier, E. L. (1982), 'Alternative multivariate tests in limited dependent variable models: an empirical assessment', *Journal of Financial and Quantitative Analysis*, vol. 17, no. 2, pp. 227–40.

Inter-American Development Bank (1984), *External Debt and Economic Development in Latin America, Background and Prospects* (Washington, DC: IADB).

International Bank for Reconstruction and Development, (1970–1980), *World Debt Tables*, on magnetic tape.

International Bank for Reconstruction and Development, (1981 and 1984), *World Debt Tables* (Washington, DC: IBRD).

IBRD (International Bank for Reconstruction and Development), (1981–1985), *World Development Report*, (Washington, DC; IBRD).

International Monetary Fund, (1948–1980), *International Financial Statistics*, on magnetic tape.

International Monetary Fund (1981a), 'External indebtedness of developing countries', International Monetary Fund Occasional Paper no. 3, Washington, DC.

International Monetary Fund (1981b, 1982a, 1984 and 1985a), *International Financial Statistics* (Washington, DC: IMF).

International Monetary Fund (1983a), 'Recent multilateral debt reschedulings with official and bank creditors', IMF Occasional Paper no. 25, Washington, DC.

International Monetary Fund (1985b), 'Recent developments in external debt restructuring' IMF Occasional Paper no. 40, Washington, DC.

International Monetary Fund (1982b, 1983b, 1985c), *World Economic Outlook* (Washington, DC: IMF).

International Monetary Fund (1985d), *World Economic Outlook: Revised Projections* (Washington, DC: IMF).

Johnson, G. G., and Abrams, R. K. (1983), 'Aspects of the international banking safety net', International Monetary Fund Occasional Papers no. 17, Washington, DC.

Judge, G. G., Hill, R. C., Griffiths, W. E., Lutkepohl, H., and Lee, T. C. (1982), *Introduction to the Theory and Practice of Econometrics* (New York: John Wiley and Sons).

Kendall, M. (1975), *Multivariate Analysis* (London: Charles Griffen & Co., Ltd).

Kindleberger, C. P. (1981), 'Debt situation of the developing countries in historical perspective (1800–1945)', *Aussenwirtschaft*, vol. 36, pp. 372–80.

King, B. B. (1968), *Notes on the Mechanics of Growth and Debt*, World Bank Staff Occasional Paper no. 6, (Baltimore, Md: Johns Hopkins Press).

Lancaster, K. J. (1966), 'A new approach to consumer theory', *Journal of Political Economy*, vol. 74, pp. 132–57.

Lancaster, K. J. (1971), *Consumer Demand: A New Approach* (New York: Columbia University Press).

Madalla, G. S. (1983), *Limited-Dependent and Qualitative Variables in Econometrics* (Cambridge: Cambridge University Press).

Maroni, Y. (1977), 'Approaches for assessing the risk involved in lending to developing countries', Board of Governors of the Federal Reserve System International Finance Discussion Papers, no. 112.

Martin, D. (1977), 'Early warning of bank failure: a logit regression approach', *Journal of Banking and Finance*, vol. 1, pp. 249–76.

Mayo, A. L. and Barret, A. G. (1977), 'An early-warning model for assessing developing-country risk', in S. H. Goodman (ed.), *Financing and Risk in Developing Countries*, (Washington, DC: Export-Import Bank), pp. 81–7.

McFadden, D. (1973), 'Conditional logit analysis of qualitative choice behaviour', in P. Zarembka, (ed.), *Frontiers in Econometrics* (New York: Academic Press), pp. 105–42.

McFadden, D. (1976), 'A comment on discriminant analysis "Versus" Logit Analysis', *Annals of Economic and Social Measurement*, vol. 5, pp. 511–23.

McFadden, D. (1981), 'Econometric models of probabilistic choice', in C. F. Manski and D. McFadden (eds.) *Structural Analysis of Discrete Data*

With Econometric Applications (Cambridge, Mass.: The MIT Press), pp. 198–272.

Mendelson, M. S. (1983), *Commercial Banks and the Restructuring of Cross-Border Debt* (New York: Group of Thirty).

Mikesell, R. F. (1962), 'The capacity to service foreign investment', in R. F. Mikesell, *U.S. Private and Government Investment Abroad* (Eugene, Oreg.: University of Oregon), pp. 377–406.

Modigliani, F., and Pogue, G. A. (1974), 'An introduction to risk and return: concepts and evidence', *Financial Analysts Journal,* March–April and May–June, pp. 68–80 and 69–86.

Mood, A., Graybill, F. and Boes, D. (1963), *Introduction to the Theory of Statistics* (New York: McGraw-Hill).

Morgan Guaranty Trust Company (1976 and 1986), 'World financial markets', July and February.

Morrison, D. F. (1976), *Multivariate Statistical Methods* (New York: McGraw-Hill).

Morrison, D. G. (1969), 'On the interpretation of discriminant analysis', *Journal of Marketing Research*, vol. 6, pp. 156–63.

Morrison, D. G. (1972), 'Upper bounds for correlations between binary outcomes and probabilistic predictions', *Journal of the American Statistical Association*, vol. 67, pp. 68–70.

Nadauld, S. D. (1981), 'Calculating the present value of an asset's uncertain future cash flows', in S. J. Maisel (ed.) *Risk and Capital Adequacy in Commercial Banks* (Chicago: The University of Chicago Press), pp. 315–39.

Organization for Economic Cooperation and Development (1979a), *Balance of Payments of OECD Countries, 1960–1979* (Paris: OECD).

Organization for Economic Cooperation and Development (1979b), *External Indebtedness of Developing Countries: Present Situation and Future Prospects* (Paris: OECD).

Organization for Economic Cooperation and Development (1982), *External Debt of Developing Countries* (Paris: OECD).

Organization for Economic Cooperation and Development (1983a), *Historical Statistics, 1960–1981* (Paris: OECD).

Organization for Economic Cooperation and Development (1983b), *Positive Adjustment Policies*, (Paris: OECD).

Park, Y. S. (1976), *Oil, Money and the World Economy*, (London: Wilton House).

Payer, C. (1974), *The Debt Trap: The International Monetary Fund and the Third World* (New York: Monthly Review Press).

Pindyck, R. S., and Rubinfeld, D. L. (1981), *Econometric Models and Economic Forecasts*, 2nd edn, (New York: McGraw-Hill).

Polak, J. J. (1948), 'Depreciation to meet a situation of overinvestment', International Monetary Fund mimeo, Washington, DC.

Porzecanski, A. C. (1980), 'The assessment of country risk: lessons from the Latin American Experience', in J.-C. Garcia-Zamor and S. E. Sutin (eds.) *Financing Development in Latin America*, (New York: Praeger Press), pp. 26–46.

Press, S. J., and Wilson, S. (1978), 'Choosing between logistic regression and discriminant analysis', *Journal of the American Statistical Association*, vol. 73, no. 364, pp. 699–705.

Robinson, P. M. (1982), 'On the asymptotic properties of estimators of models containing limited dependent variables', *Econometrica*, vol. 50, no. 1, pp. 27–41.

Rogers, J. (1983), *Global Risk Assessments: Issues, Concepts and Applications* (Riverside, Calif.: Jerry Rogers).

Sachs J. (1982a), 'The current account and macroeconomic adjustment in the 1970s', *Brookings Papers on Economic Activity*, no. 1, pp. 201–68.

Sachs, J. (1982b), 'Stabilization policies in the world economy: scope and skepticism', National Bureau of Economic Research Working Paper no. 862, Cambridge, Mass.

Sachs, J. (1982c), 'LDC debt in the 1980s: risk & reforms', National Bureau of Economic Research Working Paper no. 861, Cambridge, Mass.

Saini, K. and Bates, P. (1978), 'Statistical techniques for determining debt-servicing capacity for developing countries: analytical review of the literature and further empirical results', Federal Reserve Bank of New York Research Paper no. 7818, New York.

Sargen, N. (1977), 'Economic indicators and country risk appraisal', *Federal Reserve Bank of San Francisco Economic Review*, Fall, San Francisco, pp. 19–35.

Smith, G. W. (1975), 'Quantitative approaches to forecasting debt service problems', Mimeo, Washington, DC.

Smith, G. W. (1977), 'The external debt prospects of the non-oil exporting developing countries: an econometric analysis', Overseas Development Council NIEO Series, Monograph no. 10, Washington, DC.

Solomon, R. (1977), 'A perspective on the debt of developing countries', *Brookings Papers on Economic Activity*, no. 2, pp. 479–510.

Solomon, R. (1981), 'The debt of developing countries: another look', *Brookings Papers on Economic Activity*, no. 2, pp. 593–606.

Terrell, H. S. (1984), 'Bank lending to developing countries: recent developments and some considerations for the future', *Federal Reserve Bulletin*, vol. 70, pp. 755–63.

Theil, H. (1967), *Economics and Information Theory* (Amsterdam: North-Holland).

Theil, H. (1971), *Principles of Econometrics* (New York: John Wiley & Sons).

Truett, J., Cornfield, J., and Kannel, W. (1967), 'A multivariate analysis of the risk of coronary heart disease in Framingham', *Journal of Chronic Diseases*, vol. 20, pp. 511–24.

United Nations Committee on Trade and Development (1972), *Debt Problems of Developing Countries* (New York: The United Nations).

United Nations Committee on Trade and Development (1974), *Debt Problems in the Context of Development* (New York: The United Nations).

United Nations Committee on Trade and Development (1985), *Trade and Development Report, 1985* (New York: The United Nations).

U.S. Senate (1974), 'Report on developing countries external debt and debt relief provided by the U.S.', Washington, DC.

U.S. Senate (1975), 'Report on Debt Relief Granted by U.S. to Developing Countries', Washington, DC.

Van de Geer, J. P. (1971), *Introduction to Multivariate Analysis for the Social Sciences* (New York: W. H. Freeman & Co.)

Vernon, R. (1966), 'International investment and international trade in the product cycle', *Quarterly Journal of Economics*, vol. 80, pp. 190–207.

Villarreal, R. (1980), 'External disequilibrium in developing countries and the adjustment process: the need for a new IMF approach and policies', in J. Lozoya, and A. K. Bhattacharya (eds.) *The Financial Issues of the New International Economic Order* (New York: Pergamon Press), pp. 16–62.

The Wall Street Journal, various issues.

Walter, I. (1981), 'Country risk, portfolio decisions and regulation in international bank lending', *Journal of Banking and Finance*, vol. 5, pp. 77–92.

White, H. (1980), 'A heteroskedasticity-consistent covariance matrix estimator and a direct test for heteroskedasticity', *Econometrica*, vol. 48, no. 4, pp. 817–38.

Williamson, J. (ed.) (1983), *IMF Conditionality* (Washington, DC: Institute For International Economics).

Index